insight text guide

Robert Beardwood & Kate Macdonell

Macbeth

William Shakespeare

insight®

▸innovative ▸engaging ▸evolving

First published in 2007, reprinted 2008, 2010, 2012, 2013, 2014, 2015 (twice), 2016, 2017, 2018, 2020, 2021, 2023, 2024, 2025.

Insight Publications Pty Ltd
3/350 Charman Road
Cheltenham VIC 3192
Australia
Tel: +61 3 8571 4950
Email: books@insightpublications.com.au

www.insightpublications.com.au

National Library of Australia Cataloguing-in-Publication entry:
Beardwood, Robert, 1966–.
William Shakespeare's Macbeth: text guide.
Bibliography.
For secondary and tertiary students.
9781921088605 (pbk.).
1. Shakespeare, William, 1564–1616. Macbeth – Criticism and interpretation.
I. Macdonell, Kate. II. Title.
822.33T6

Other ISBNs:
9781925175141 (digital)

Cover design: Modern Art Production Group

Proudly Printed in Australia by Ligare Book Printers

Insight Publications acknowledges the Traditional Custodians of the Country on which we meet and work, the Boonwurrung People of the Kulin Nation. We pay our respects to their Elders past and present, and extend that respect to all Aboriginal and Torres Strait Islander peoples.

contents

CHARACTER MAP

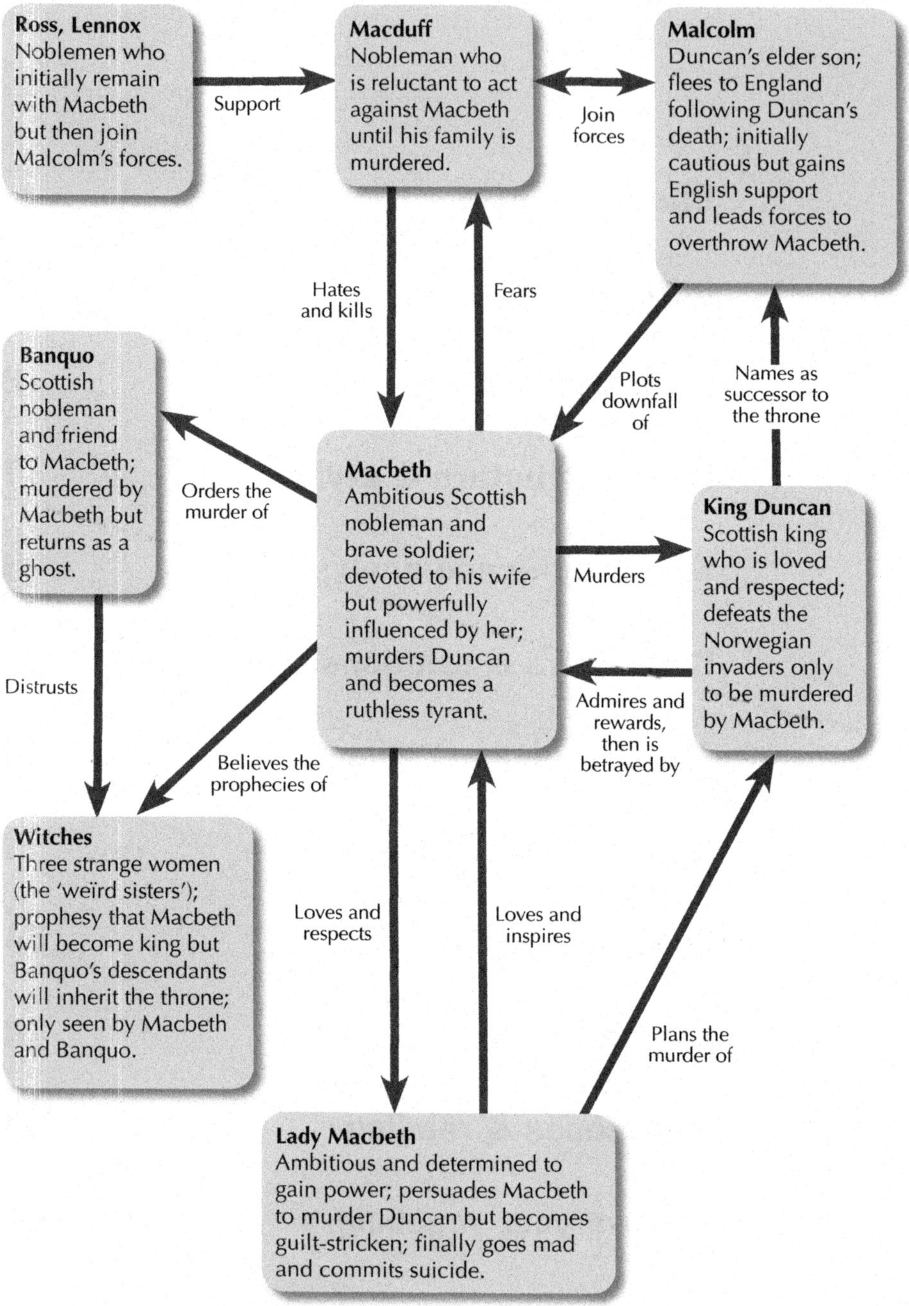

INTRODUCTION

Macbeth is one of the best-known and most admired plays in the English language. It continues to be performed and studied around the world; contemporary film and television adaptations, some using the original dialogue and others rewriting the script, convey the story to new generations and audiences.

Set in eleventh-century Scotland, Shakespeare's account of an ambitious nobleman spurred on by his wife to grab power by force and to rule by terror has always resonated with audiences and readers. It is a play of relentless tension and violence: several characters die onstage, and countless other deaths are graphically described or nervously hinted at. Images of blood pervade the play, from Macbeth's sword that 'smok'd with bloody execution' (1.2.18) to his vision of a dagger with 'gouts of blood' and Malcolm's despairing summary of Scotland's state: 'It weeps, it bleeds, and each new day a gash / Is added to her wounds' (4.3.40–1). Blood becomes the very element in which Macbeth lives and breathes.

Threaded through this drama of violent action and ruthless scheming is an atmosphere of uncertainty and confusion, in which opposites merge and boundaries dissolve. Witches, appearing as if from nowhere and then disappearing into thin air, prophesy events that seem improbable, but eerily become reality. Characters echo one another or uncannily predict their own fates. Lady Macbeth urges her husband not to reflect on Duncan's murder or 'it will make us mad' (2.2.37) – and so it does, though their madness manifests in opposite, yet equally devastating, ways.

Behind *Macbeth*'s tense action and atmosphere is the discomforting idea that our lives are not merely our own, but are mapped out by forces beyond our control and comprehension. Each character resists this notion in their own way, yet each is caught up in a larger pattern of events over which they have little control. As much as *Macbeth* is a play of violent action, it is also a play of intense introspection: it is an account of a tyrant that becomes an extended meditation on the nature of power and even on the meaning of life. Macbeth commits the play's most heinous acts, but he also expresses the most complex understanding of his place in the larger scheme of things and – albeit too late – of his own mortality and inevitable fate.

him at the banquet. Macbeth now commits himself to a path of violence, seeing himself as being at a point of no return ('Returning were as tedious as go o'er', 3.4.138). Finally Malcolm, the rightful heir to the throne, leads a successful challenge to Macbeth's rule, and order is restored to Scotland.

Fear, or horror, is aroused by the ruthlessness with which Macbeth and Lady Macbeth (who is also a tragic figure) pursue their ambition, and by the murder of innocents, climaxing in the slaughter of Lady Macduff and her children. Pity for the protagonists is less readily experienced until the fifth act, when Lady Macbeth's sleepwalking scene and Macbeth's last speeches show both to have achieved some recognition of the true nature of their actions.

Five-act structure: rising then falling action

The five acts of *Macbeth* – like those of Shakespeare's other tragedies – follow a standard pattern, with the tension rising through the first half of the play, then falling in the second half as the hero's fortunes decline.

Structural role	Action in *Macbeth*
Act 1 The exposition: the scene is set	• Norwegian forces defeated • Macbeth acclaimed and rewarded • Macbeth and Banquo meet the witches • Macbeth and Lady Macbeth resolve to murder Duncan
Act 2 The tension increases	• Duncan's murder (followed by a comic interlude, the Porter's speech, briefly relieving the tension) • Malcolm and Donaldbain flee; Macbeth becomes king
Act 3 The tension reaches a climax; the hero faces a crisis and is increasingly isolated from others	• Banquo is murdered, then his ghost appears before Macbeth at a royal banquet • Macbeth realises that peace is now unattainable, and commits himself to violent rule
Act 4 The start of the hero's declining power; opposing forces gather strength	• Macbeth returns to the witches; he orders the slaughter of Macduff's family • Malcolm, gathering forces in England, meets Macduff and gains his support
Act 5 The hero's downfall and death; the resolution of the conflict	• Lady Macbeth, now mad, sleepwalks then commits suicide • The English forces and rebel Scottish lords advance on Macbeth's castle • Macduff fights and kills Macbeth; Malcolm becomes king

Patterns of imagery

One of the most striking features of *Macbeth* is its rich use of recurring images. These patterns of imagery give the play a strong sense of unity, and convey many of the play's central ideas as well as creating atmosphere and tension.

Images of blood

The most dominant of these patterns of imagery is that of blood, reflecting the prevalence of violence, especially under Macbeth's rule. Macbeth seems inextricably linked with blood shed in violent acts, from his sword which 'smok'd with bloody execution' (1.2.18) to the 'gouts of blood' on the dagger he imagines seeing (2.1.46) and Banquo's 'gory locks' (3.4.51).

If blood imagery conveys the pervasive violence of Macbeth's rule, it also creates a sense of how appalled Macbeth himself is by what he has done. When he thinks of Duncan's blood on his hands it seems sufficient to turn the 'multitudinous seas' red (2.2.65). Of course, it is the magnitude of the crime, not the physical quantity of blood that makes sense of this image. Later he imagines himself wading into a river or lake not merely coloured by blood but *made* of it, into which were he to 'wade no more, / Returning were as tedious as go o'er' (3.4.136–8). Macbeth explains here that he has waded so far through blood that it is as difficult to return as it is to keep going – so he resolves to continue with his murderous rampage. Lady Macbeth, too, reaches a psychological point of no return, when she is utterly unable to remove the stain of blood from her mind: 'Here's the smell of the blood still', she laments (5.1.44).

Blood also signifies kinship, and images of blood shed in violence also reflect the ways in which Macbeth ruthlessly severs family bonds. He robs Malcolm, Donaldbain and Fleance of their fathers; he dispossesses Macduff of his entire family. Indeed, Macbeth's first words to Donaldbain and Malcolm after Duncan's body is discovered point to this link between the shedding of blood and the destruction of families: 'the fountain of your blood / Is stopp'd' (2.3.94–5). It is the destruction of family as much as the loss of individual human life that marks Macbeth as a tyrant whose deeds threaten the values and ties that bind society together.

Images of ill-fitting clothes

Just as the image of blood is clearly related to the exploration of violent rule in *Macbeth*, clothes that are ill-fitting are strongly linked to the theme of deceptive appearances (see 'Themes, Ideas & Values'). Clothes are used in *Macbeth* as a metaphor for the self that characters present to the world; they can also signify social standing or title. The image of ill-fitting clothes, then, is a metaphor for the gap between a character's outward or public persona and their inner reality – their real thoughts and feelings.

Macbeth, who spends much of the first half of the play attempting to conceal his underlying desires, is often described as wearing 'clothes' that are ill-fitting. When he is awarded the title of Thane of Cawdor, he wonders why he is dressed 'In borrow'd robes' (1.3.106–7), and Banquo suggests that his 'New honours' are 'Like our strange garments [that] cleave not to their mould, / But with the aid of use' (1.3.143–5). That is, Banquo perceives that Macbeth needs time to become accustomed to his elevated status, and even Macbeth realises that the 'golden opinions' he has received should be 'worn now in their newest gloss, / Not cast aside so soon' (1.7.32–5). However, Macbeth does not allow himself 'the aid of use', but proceeds impulsively to acquire greater power. As a result, he is constantly presenting a public self to the world that diverges significantly from his inner self.

Macbeth's discomfort in his official role is emphasised again near the play's end, as the rebel Scottish lords observe that Macbeth feels 'his title / Hang loose about him, like a giant's robe / Upon a dwarfish thief' (5.2.20–2). By this time, of course, Macbeth has abandoned any attempt to conceal his true nature from others. As he prepares to defend his castle he once more puts on his soldier's armour, and regains something of the stature and nobility he had at the beginning.

Images of nature

Throughout *Macbeth*, images of the natural world form a counterpart to events that take place in the world of men and women – the world of society, politics, families and the fluctuating fortunes of individual lives. As the Doctor plainly states – in relation to Lady Macbeth's madness, but pertinent to the play's events overall – 'unnatural deeds / Do breed unnatural troubles' (5.1.63–4). In this way, nature is seen as holding up a mirror to society; the broad repercussions of a single destructive human action are conveyed through images of the parallel discord in the world of nature.

Just as Duncan's murder inverts the conventional social order, the natural order too seems to be inverted, such that Duncan's horses 'Turn'd wild in nature' (2.4.16) and a falcon 'Was by a mousing owl hawk'd at and kill'd' (2.4.13). Thus, Duncan's murder is portrayed not simply as a blow struck against an individual, or even the monarchy, but as a corruption of an entire world, natural as well as social.

References to birds are always significant in *Macbeth*, and they fall into two main groups:

- One group associates birds with family integrity and loyalty; for example, Banquo describes the 'temple-haunting martlet[s]' at Inverness (1.6.4), and Lady Macduff invokes 'the poor wren' that 'will fight, / Her young ones in her nest, against the owl' (4.2.9–11).
- The second group of bird images are those of black birds, signs of imminent violence or death; for example, Lady Macbeth declares that 'The raven himself is hoarse / That croaks the fatal entrance of Duncan' (1.5.37–8), and Macbeth looks forward to the time of day when 'the crow makes wing to th'rooky wood' and 'night's black agents to their preys do rouse' (3.2.47–53).

Animals that scuttle or slither along the ground are also used to suggest sinister intentions and a sense of foreboding. Snakes and scorpions signify danger and treachery: for example, Lady Macbeth recommends that she and Macbeth maintain a welcoming appearance but 'be the serpent under't' (1.5.65). The effect of behaving in this way, though, is to create a permanently uneasy state of mind – as if the 'serpent', once within, is impossible to remove. Macbeth complains, 'We have scorch'd the snake, not kill'd it' (3.2.13) and asserts his mind is 'full of scorpions' (3.2.36), conveying his disquiet as well his lethal intent.

Images of order and disorder

As the above discussion of natural imagery makes clear, the extent of the disorder and violence in Macbeth's Scotland is conveyed by images of natural phenomena that are either extremely unnatural or deeply foreboding.

Another recurring image that suggests how order is overthrown by disorder is that of the banquet – which, in a conventionally functioning society, suggests order and peace in human affairs. Even Macbeth desires such a state when he greets his guests with: 'You know your own degrees, sit down; at first and last, the hearty welcome' (3.4.1–2). However, the banquet turns into an embarrassing disaster when Banquo's ghost appears before Macbeth; if Macbeth has murdered sleep, he has also made it impossible to share a meal in peace.

Thus, Macbeth despairs that he and Lady Macbeth must now 'eat our meal in fear' (3.2.17), and he forces the rest of Scotland to experience this fear, too. The Lord who speaks with Lennox hopes Macduff's actions will 'Free from our feasts and banquets bloody knives' (3.6.35): Macbeth has destroyed, by implication, all such innocent and everyday pleasures.

- Another important set of images conveying the state of disorder in Scotland under Macbeth's reign are those of infection and disease. Look for instances of these and think about how they present the ideas of disorder and corruption.

Images of light and dark

Images of light and dark represent forces of good and evil respectively. Duncan, for instance, aligns stars with goodness and nobility, hoping that 'signs of nobleness like stars shall shine / On all deservers' (1.4.41–2). Macbeth, though, appeals to the heavens to conceal sources of light: 'Stars, hide your fires, / Let not light see my black and deep desires' (1.4.50–1).

The witches are clearly associated with darkness. Banquo suggests they are 'instruments of darkness' (1.3.123), and Macbeth greets them as 'secret, black, and midnight hags' (4.1.47). Both Macbeth and Lady Macbeth invoke darkness to help them fulfil the witches' prophecies. In an uncanny echo of her husband, Lady Macbeth summons 'thick night' so that heaven cannot witness her actions (1.5.49–52), a plea that seems to be answered when Banquo suggests that 'There's husbandry in heaven, / Their candles are all out' (2.1.4–5). This marks the beginning of a long period of darkness for Scotland, the end of which only appears imminent when Malcolm declares: 'The night is long that never finds the day' (4.3.243).

The reign of terror and uncertainty in Scotland is reflected in the inversion of light and dark. Ross observes that 'By th'clock 'tis day / And yet dark night strangles the travelling lamp' (2.4.6–7). Conversely, Lady Macbeth becomes terrified of darkness and keeps a lighted candle by her throughout the night – which fails, however, to keep her terrible thoughts suppressed (5.1).

Soliloquies and asides

These two kinds of speeches allow for the expression of a character's true feelings, and in *Macbeth* they are crucial to the audience's understanding of character motivations and intentions. *Soliloquies* are delivered with no other character onstage, such as Macbeth's 'If it were done when 'tis done' (1.7.1–28). These are usually longer than asides, and allow the character to reflect on a dilemma or crisis that confronts them.

Asides are also important and take place while other characters remain onstage, although without hearing what the speaking character says. An example occurs when Macbeth learns from Ross that he will be the next Thane of Cawdor, and then informs the audience that his thoughts are far more treacherous than the other characters suspect (1.3.127–46).

These theatrical conventions are very important in *Macbeth* for their role in developing the two principal characters. Both Macbeth and Lady Macbeth often seek to conceal their true selves from others, so their admission of their real thoughts and feelings to the audience is essential for understanding their complex inner lives.

Poetry and prose

Most of *Macbeth* is written in **blank verse**, the standard poetic form used by Elizabethan playwrights. This means that each line is ten syllables in length and has an alternating pattern of stressed (or emphasised) and unstressed syllables.

For example, in Macbeth's first line we show the stressed syllables in bold:

So **foul** and **fair** a **day** I **have** not **seen**.

Each pair of unstressed and stressed syllables comprises one metrical unit, known as a 'foot': thus, there are five 'feet' in each line. The foot which has an unstressed followed by a stressed syllable is called an *iamb* (pronounced 'I-Am'), and the rhythmic pattern with five iambs per line is called *iambic pentameter*.

Rhyme

Blank verse is unrhymed, so the occasions on which Shakespeare uses rhyme are unusual, and therefore significant. For example, much of the witches' dialogue is in rhyming couplets, giving their speech an incantatory (chanting) quality even when they are not casting a spell. Macbeth generates a similar feeling when he ends a speech with a rhyming couplet:

Come what come may,
Time and the hour runs through the roughest day (1.3.145–6).

Shakespeare also uses rhyming couplets at the ends of scenes to generate a sense of closure. An example in *Macbeth* occurs at the end of Act 4, when Malcolm declares he will lead the army to attack Macbeth:

Receive what cheer you may:
The night is long that never finds the day.

Prose

Sometimes a character's lines are written in prose rather than poetry. This is usually the case when the character is not a member of the nobility – the Porter is the most notable case in *Macbeth* (2.3), but other examples include the Doctor and Gentlewoman (5.1).

Macbeth and Lady Macbeth also have their lines written in prose at key points in the text, conveying their altered states of mind. In Act 3 Scene 1, Macbeth initially speaks to the Murderers in prose, tentatively sounding out their thoughts and feelings – this is, after all, the first occasion on which he hires men to commit murder. Then, as he becomes surer of their allegiance to him, his speech becomes more confident and adopts the regular rhythms of blank verse.

Lady Macbeth's dialogue in Act 5 Scene 1 is also written as prose rather than poetry. The regular pattern and rhythmic flow of blank verse is replaced by prose made up of fragments ('One, two'), repeated words ('come') and sounds ('O'), exclamations and unanswerable questions. The lack of coherence in her speech as she leaps from one appalling thought to another conveys her deranged and tortured state of mind, although the meaning of what she says is all too clear to the audience.

Irony and echo

Many words and phrases recur in *Macbeth*, often spoken by different characters. These add to the atmosphere of unease and foreboding, as if supernatural forces are indeed influencing characters' thoughts and actions. At other times, a sense of threat is created by dramatic irony: the full meaning or significance of a character's statement is understood by the audience but not by the character.

These two techniques can coincide, as when Macbeth's first line – 'So foul and fair a day I have not seen' (1.3.36) – echoes the witches' 'Fair is foul, and foul is fair' (1.1.12). The audience knows what the witches have said, but Macbeth does not; the echo suggests that we are about to see Macbeth being drawn unwittingly into the witches' 'plot'.

At other times, a character is simply unaware of what is being planned by those around them, and their words betray their ignorance. Duncan says 'There's no art / To find the mind's construction in the face (1.4.11–12), but he is more right than he realises. Macbeth speaks falsely throughout this scene, which *we* are aware of. Duncan, however, proceeds to place an 'absolute trust' in Macbeth, as he had with the previous Thane of Cawdor, and does not suspect that Macbeth has ulterior motives.

Lady Macbeth's decline from sanity into madness is marked by several echoes in her sleepwalking scene (Act 5 Scene 1). Her confident, 'A little water clears us of this deed' (2.2.70) pre-empts her ceaseless hand-wringing as she asks herself, 'will these hands ne'er be clean?' (5.1.39). Similarly, 'what's done, is done' (3.2.12), conveying her determination to move forward, is transformed into the far more regretful, 'what's done cannot be undone' (5.1.59–60). Finally, her advice to Macbeth not to reflect on the murder since 'it will make us mad' (2.2.36–7) is revealed to be tragically prophetic.

SCENE-BY-SCENE ANALYSIS

Act 1 Scene 1

Summary: *Three witches meet in an open field during a storm.*

The opening scene introduces the three witches and the idea of their influence on Macbeth's tragic demise. The Third Witch's knowledge of when the battle will end between the army of King Duncan and the rebel and Norwegian forces – 'ere the set of sun' (line 5) – shows the knowledge these characters have of human affairs. Moreover, their intention to overturn the natural order is clearly signalled by the closing chant: 'Fair is foul, and foul is fair' (line 12).

Q Do the witches seem to be women with strange powers or supernatural creatures?

Act 1 Scene 2

Summary: *A Captain tells Duncan about Macbeth's efforts in battle; Duncan decides to make Macbeth the new Thane of Cawdor.*

Macbeth's prowess on the battlefield and his loyalty to Duncan are highlighted in this scene. The Captain's depiction of Macbeth's vigorous assault on Macdonald, whom Macbeth has 'unseam'd … from the nave to th'chaps' (line 22) and promptly decapitated, shows the ruthlessness with which he disposes of an enemy. Ross's story about the fight between Macbeth and the traitorous Cawdor confirms Macbeth's unmitigated bravery in battle. Duncan decides to reward Macbeth by making him the new Thane of Cawdor – this validates the witches' prophecy in the following scene.

Key point

The imagery of clothing is introduced in this scene (see Genre, structure & style). The 'unseam[ing]' of Macdonald signals how easily the fabric of a traitorous body can be undone; in contrast, Macbeth's body is wrapped in good armour – 'lapp'd in proof' (line 54) – suggesting his actions are honourable.

Q Identify the references to blood in this scene. What do they suggest about Macbeth?

Act 1 Scene 3

Summary: *The witches relate prophecies to Macbeth and Banquo.*

This key scene is crucial to understanding both the power of the witches and Macbeth's vulnerability to them. The detail with which they plot the demise of a sailor establishes their malevolence (evil), and their 'wither'd', 'wild' (line 38) and unfeminine appearance, which initially bewilders Banquo, suggests their unnatural, otherworldly status.

Banquo's initial confusion, however, gives way to a rationality that Macbeth lacks. Whereas Macbeth is startled by being addressed as Thane of Cawdor and by the prophecy that he will become 'king hereafter' (line 48), Banquo treats his prospects of being one who 'shalt get kings' (line 65) with circumspection. He advises Macbeth to be wary of what he has heard when Ross delivers the news to Macbeth that he has indeed been named Thane of Cawdor.

Despite this warning, Macbeth's thoughts soon turn to murder: his reactions demonstrate the precarious grip he has on his emotions. Although appearing ready to allow chance to bring him to the throne, his request to Banquo that they later discuss their encounter with the witches reveals his inability to let the matter rest. Further, his attempt to make light of his reverie to Banquo, Ross and Angus establishes Macbeth's ability and willingness to hide his true feelings.

Q What are the similarities and differences between Banquo and Macbeth in this scene? Find evidence (including stage directions) to support your views.

Act 1 Scene 4

Summary: *Duncan announces Malcolm as his successor; Macbeth leaves for Inverness to prepare for Duncan's arrival.*

Macbeth becomes increasingly preoccupied with hiding his true feelings in this scene and throughout Act 1. Here, however, it is not only Macbeth whose appearance is recognised as deceptive. The former Thane of Cawdor is recognised by Duncan as having once been 'a gentleman on whom I built / An absolute trust' (lines 13–14). It is ironic, therefore, that Duncan's understanding of the difficulties involved in reading 'the mind's construction in the face' (line 12) does little to prevent his blind faith in Macbeth's loyalty. Macbeth's claim of duty to Duncan's 'throne and state' (line 25) is clearly disingenuous (dishonest) given his earlier thoughts of murder. Macbeth's calm response to Duncan's announcement that Malcolm will succeed him also masks his true feelings, which are subsequently revealed to the audience in an aside.

Q Macbeth's aside comprises three sets of rhyming couplets (*aa-bb-cc*). Where else in the play are similar rhyme schemes used? What does this suggest about Macbeth's state of mind at this point in the play?

Act 1 Scene 5

Summary: *Lady Macbeth receives a letter from Macbeth describing the prophecies; she plans for Duncan's murder.*

This short scene explores the relationship between Lady Macbeth and her husband, illustrating ways in which their personalities are both similar and different.

Macbeth's letter is remarkable for its directness and for the intimate way it involves Lady Macbeth in the prospect of future glory. His reference to his wife as his 'dearest partner of greatness' (line 10) demonstrates his regard for her as an equal; his request that she 'lay' his news 'to thy heart' (lines 12–13) shows his candour and trust in her.

These positive attributes are consolidated by Lady Macbeth's depiction of his honourable nature. Although she regards this as a weakness, it is precisely Macbeth's broad emotional range that makes him a tragic figure, and initially Lady Macbeth is a far less sympathetic figure. She is confident of her influence over Macbeth and knows that 'the valour of [her] tongue' (line 26) will overcome his moral scruples.

Lady Macbeth's pragmatic and determined approach to success is at odds with Macbeth's more hesitant, uncertain style. Lady Macbeth's assurance, however, belies (conceals) a fear of her own vulnerability. Like Macbeth, when she contemplates murder she too hopes that her 'keen knife not see the wound it makes' (line 51; compare Macbeth at 1.5.51–2). Unlike him, though, she invokes the forces of darkness to rid her of all feminine traits. Although her invocation to the spirits is commanding, the detail with which Lady Macbeth lists her potential weaknesses illustrates her determination to suppress her own better impulses.

Q How do Macbeth and Lady Macbeth interact in this scene? Note any differences in the way Macbeth communicates in writing and in person.

Act 1 Scene 6

Summary: *Duncan and his followers arrive at Macbeth's castle.*

Although this scene contains many images of harmony and honour in relationships, it is heavily ironic.

Duncan's comments to Banquo about the peaceful setting of the castle are imbued with dramatic irony given the discussion of regicide in the previous scene. This tension is further heightened by Banquo's comments about the numerous nests on the castle built by the 'temple-haunting martlet' (line 4). Banquo's implication is that this is a good place for families, which is ironic given Macbeth's later acts of violence that destroy family units.

Key point

Note the deferential conduct of Lady Macbeth towards Duncan in this scene. She has clearly taken her own advice of looking 'like th'innocent flower' but being 'the serpent under't' (1.5.64–5).

Q Explain the irony of Duncan's comment to Lady Macbeth that he and his men had 'cours'd' (or chased, as when animals are hunted) Macbeth to Inverness.

Act 1 Scene 7

Summary: *Macbeth ponders the negative consequences of murdering Duncan but Lady Macbeth persuades him to proceed.*

This scene opens with Macbeth in soliloquy, reflecting on three main anxieties he has about murdering Duncan:

- Macbeth is aware of the negative impact of the murder on his chances of being contented in the after-life ('the life to come', line 7) and also in his lifetime. Macbeth understands that 'Bloody instructions ... being taught, return / To plague th'inventor' (lines 9–10). This anxiety is self-directed – it concerns the impact of the crime on Macbeth himself.

- Macbeth understands that the murder is a violation of the moral order. He believes that pity will 'blow the horrid deed in every eye' (line 24) since the murder would subvert his moral obligations to the king as his relative, subject and host.
- Macbeth also reveals his anxieties about the true nature of his ambition – that it is so excessive that it 'o'erleaps itself' (line 27) and will ultimately cause his downfall.

Although these anxieties dissuade Macbeth from committing the murder, they are soon dispelled by the persuasive powers of Lady Macbeth. She dismisses his appeal to honour, questioning his masculinity and then accusing him of breaking a promise. Her insistence that she would have murdered her own child if she had promised to conveys her desperate desire to secure the crown. Just as previously she invoked spirits to 'unsex' her (1.5.40), in this scene too Lady Macbeth rejects conventional notions of how women should act and feel, in order to become queen.

Q Do you view Macbeth more sympathetically or less after this scene? Why?

Act 2 Scene 1

Summary: *Banquo has a sense of foreboding; Macbeth has a vision of a dagger, then goes to Duncan's chamber.*

This scene initially explores Banquo's feelings of unease as the play's dramatic tension increases. His foreboding parallels the anxiety Macbeth has about the murder he is about to commit. However, while Banquo's concerns manifest themselves in a fear of going to sleep, Macbeth's disquietude results in hallucination.

Key point

Banquo's comment to Fleance that 'There's husbandry in heaven, / Their candles are all out' (lines 4–5) suggests that Macbeth and Lady Macbeth's earlier pleas for darkness to hide their actions have been successful.

Macbeth's soliloquy, which describes his vision of a dagger leading the way towards Duncan's chamber, conveys Macbeth's uneasy state of mind and also foreshadows his murder of Duncan. The appearance of 'gouts of blood' confirms Macbeth's sense that the vision arises from his preoccupation with 'the bloody business' (line 48). Despite the intensity of the vision and the shocking violence it intimates, Macbeth carries out the murder. He notes that threats are no substitute for action – anticipating his later insistence on acting without thinking.

Q Explain how the image of 'wither'd murder … towards his design / Moves like a ghost' (lines 52–6) conveys Macbeth's view of himself at this point.

Act 2 Scene 2

Summary: *Macbeth is unnerved by the murder he has committed; Lady Macbeth attempts to reassure him.*

While the play does not depict the actual murder of Duncan, this scene is nonetheless harrowing for the way in which it conveys Macbeth's deep remorse for killing Duncan. It also shows Lady Macbeth's own emotional fragility and her attempts to mask it from her husband.

Although Lady Macbeth spikes the chamberlains' drinks and lays out their daggers, she is far from the 'fiend' (5.9.36) Malcolm ultimately describes her as. The fact that she must drink alcohol to become sufficiently 'bold' (line 1) to be an accomplice to murder suggests that she is not an innately ruthless character. She reflects that she would have committed the murder had Duncan not resembled her father, revealing that she experiences a wider range of emotions than she shows to her husband, as does her agitated demeanour while she awaits Macbeth's return.

This nervousness informs the interaction between Lady Macbeth and Macbeth: note the short, sharp dialogue that reveals their anxieties. Unlike Macbeth, however, Lady Macbeth composes herself and endeavours to quell his fears. She tells him 'These deeds must not be thought / After these ways; so, it will make us mad' (lines 36–7), and declares: 'A little water clears us of this deed' (line 70). Of course, Lady Macbeth's advice to Macbeth ironically becomes advice she is unable to apply herself. Certainly her admonishment of Macbeth's pallor after she returns the daggers indicates a strength of mind that she will not keep.

Q How is Macbeth's remorse for killing Duncan signposted in this scene?

Act 2 Scene 3

Summary: *The Porter converses with Macduff who has arrived to wake Duncan; Macduff discovers Duncan's body; Macbeth appears grieved; Duncan's sons flee.*

This scene opens with the castle's porter opening the gates to Macduff and Lennox. The Porter is drunk and his style of speech is casual and sexually provocative, demonstrating his loose grip on propriety in his inebriated state. Note how he also speaks in prose rather than verse, which further shows his low social standing and lack of decorum. His sense that he is the keeper of the gates of hell is particularly ironic given the murder that has taken place.

Whereas the Porter's scene provides some relief from the intensity of the previous scene, Lennox's comments about the wildness of the night and Macbeth's guilt-ridden reticence when Macduff asks after the king create an overwhelming feeling of disquiet. This is exacerbated by Macduff's discovery of Duncan's corpse and Macbeth's corresponding verbosity as he expresses his feelings – partly feigned, and partly real – of loss and anger.

Macbeth's speech is unnerving precisely because it is so excessive and uncontrolled. Although Macbeth is partly acting to deceive the others, his comment that 'the mere lees' of life are all that are left now that 'grace is dead' (lines 90–1) betrays his understanding that he has killed more than simply a person. However, when he unconvincingly tries to justify murdering the groomsmen, the extravagance and hypocrisy of his language, combined with his uncannily detailed description of Duncan's body, causes Lady Macbeth to faint – possibly to deflect attention from her husband, or perhaps from real shock at these additional murders. Her action allows Banquo to calm things down, and Macbeth's speech is terse for the remainder of the scene.

Duncan's sons, Malcolm and Donaldbain, are reluctant to speak: their silence reflects their real state of shock, in contrast to Macbeth's deliberate protests. They recognise that it is now impossible to know who to trust – 'There's daggers in men's smiles' (lines 136–7) – leading Malcolm to flee to England and Donaldbain to seek safety in Ireland.

Q Do you find Macbeth's speeches convincing (lines 87–92 and 104–14)? Or are they clearly attempts to *pretend* to be upset? Explain your response.

Act 2 Scene 4

Summary: *Ross and the Old Man discuss the strange occurrences paralleling Duncan's death.*

This scene describes the overturning of the natural order that occurs in conjunction with Duncan's murder, a sign that the heavens are 'troubled with man's act' (line 5).

The account of disorder in the natural world leads into the discussion with Macduff about the social order being disrupted. Macduff's claim that the groomsmen killed Duncan after being 'suborn'd' by Malcolm and Donaldbain is represented as ''Gainst nature' (line 27) by Ross. However, Macduff's decision to return to his castle at Fife, rather than go to Scone for Macbeth's coronation, intimates (suggests) his own unease about Macbeth's involvement.

Q Explain the meaning of Macduff's comment 'Lest our old robes sit easier than our new' (line 38). What does this suggest about Macduff's character?

Key point

Note how this scene brings Act 2 to a close by reflecting on and, importantly, drawing back from, the action that has occurred in the preceding scenes. This reflective quality encourages us to see the wider ramifications of Macbeth's actions – just as a similar scene does at the end of Act 3.

Act 3 Scene 1

Summary: *Macbeth orders two men to murder Banquo and his son, Fleance.*

This scene, like Act 3 generally, focuses on the idea of fear and how it manifests itself in different characters.

Banquo's soliloquy expresses his fear that Macbeth has 'played'st most foully' (line 3), but Banquo muses only briefly on the witches' claim that he will be the 'root and father / Of many kings' (lines 5–6) before dismissing such speculation. Like Macbeth, he is hopeful; unlike Macbeth, he is not murderous.

Macbeth's fear of Banquo's descendants becoming kings so disturbs him that he claims it is merely 'For them' that he has murdered Duncan and 'Put rancours in the vessel' of his peace (lines 67–8). Macbeth's unease is also evident in the negative way he describes the accoutrements (trappings) associated with being king: he believes he wears 'a fruitless crown' and holds 'a barren sceptre', which will eventually be 'wrenched' from him (lines 62–4). Given that Macbeth has 'wrenched' the crown from Duncan, his 'fears in Banquo' (line 50) are extremely hypocritical.

Macbeth's fears propel him to act – he arranges the murders of Banquo and Fleance, without any sign of hesitation or self-doubt. The urgency with which he charges the murderers to kill that evening, combined with his insistence that his own complicity in the crime not be discovered, underscore the way fear informs his actions.

Q Explain the irony of Macbeth's insistence to Banquo that he 'Fail not our feast' (line 29) in the light of what actually happens at the banquet.

Act 3 Scene 2

Summary: *Macbeth and Lady Macbeth discuss their lack of contentment.*

This scene charts Macbeth and Lady Macbeth's responses to the emotional consequences of murdering Duncan. Lady Macbeth's acknowledgement that 'our desire is got without content' (line 5) and advice to Macbeth that 'what's done, is done' (line 12) mark a shift in her personality. Whereas previously she was ambitious, she now appears to quietly accept the consequences of her actions.

In contrast, Macbeth's emotional response to his situation is varied and complex, as he shifts between despair and defiance. Believing that he can improve things by committing further evil acts, he further immerses himself in a world of violence and deceit.

Q Re-read Act 1 Scene 5. How have the personalities and language of Macbeth and Lady Macbeth changed since that scene?

Act 3 Scene 3

Summary: *The murderers kill Banquo but Fleance escapes.*

Macbeth's insecurity about the murderers' competence leads him to hire another as reinforcement. The Third Murderer appears to be more canny than the other two: he is alert to the sound of horses, for instance, and recognises Banquo's face. He does not expect the light to be struck out and implies that the darkness is precisely what allows Fleance to escape.

Act 3 Scene 4

Summary: *Macbeth is disheartened by the news of Fleance's escape; Banquo's ghost appears to Macbeth at the banquet.*

The bloodied ghost of Banquo unnerves Macbeth, whose odd behaviour compels Lady Macbeth to rationalise it to the guests and question Macbeth's manhood in private. Unlike her previous attempt to strengthen his resolve in this way (1.7.49–51), this time she is unable to control Macbeth and ultimately requests that the guests leave. This is the second (and last) time she 'saves' Macbeth by deflecting attention from him.

Macbeth now becomes unconcerned about whether others discover his crimes, and resolves to act without hesitation. He accepts that he will commit more murders, believing that he is now so much 'in blood' (line 136) that returning to a more innocent life is impossible. This marks an important turning point: any possibility that Macbeth might restore peaceful rule to Scotland has now vanished.

Q How significant is it that Banquo's ghost is only visible to Macbeth? Could it be just another vision (like the dagger) or is it more 'real' than this?

Act 3 Scene 5

Summary: *Hecate chastises the witches and plans to bring about Macbeth's destruction.*

Most experts agree that this scene was not written by Shakespeare. Nonetheless, the scene provides a glimpse into the scheming nature of the witches. Hecate's admonishment of the other witches for not including her in their mischief-making motivates her to plot a final display of 'artificial sprites' which will draw Macbeth on and bring about his downfall.

Act 3 Scene 6

Summary: *Lennox and an unnamed Lord discuss the state of Scotland.*

The sarcastic tenor (tone) of Lennox's speech to the Lord clearly shows that his allegiance is no longer to Macbeth. He is suspicious of Macbeth's apparent grief after Duncan's death and the convenient slaying of the groomsmen. His acrimonious reference to Macbeth as the 'tyrant' and his understanding that he must be careful of what he says shows that Macbeth's is a reign of terror.

Both men understand that Macduff's opposition to Macbeth and his refusal to meet with the tyrant mark him as a potential victim.

Key point

The Lord's comments about the 'bloody knives' at banquets and the lack of sleep endured by the Scottish people echoes Macbeth's earlier assertion that others would have to endure these things before he puts up with them himself (see 3.2.16–19).

Q How does this scene position us to think about the previously minor characters Macduff and Malcolm?

Act 4 Scene 1

Summary: *Macbeth meets with the witches.*

Macbeth's yearning to know his fate compels him to see the witches once more. He hears the apparitions without being alert to the ambiguities of their prophecies – his overly literal mind leads him to 'read' their words and images in ways favourable to himself. His resolve to nevertheless 'make assurance double sure' (line 82) by killing Macduff is foiled by the latter's timely flight to England. This event sends a clear signal to the audience that Macduff will indeed be Macbeth's nemesis.

Macduff's flight, in conjunction with the witches' confirmation that Banquo's descendants shall become kings, drives Macbeth to impose an even greater reign of terror on his subjects. His impulsive and vindictive decision to slaughter every member of Macduff's family demonstrates how completely unconscionable Macbeth's behaviour has become.

Act 4 Scene 2

Summary: *Lady Macduff reflects on Macduff's absence; she and her children are murdered by Macbeth's henchmen.*

Although this scene ends in brutal murder, its early lines are remarkably gentle in tone. Lady Macduff despairs at her husband's insensitivity and

Ross finds it difficult to maintain his composure. The moving nature of these lines gives way (following Ross's departure) to light banter between Lady Macduff and her son – the tone of this exchange serves as a foil for the ensuing terror, heightening the dramatic impact of the murders.

Q Is Macduff's decision to leave his family without providing them with any protection justified in your view?

Act 4 Scene 3

Summary: *At the English court, Macduff tries to persuade Malcolm to return to Scotland; Macduff learns of his family's demise.*

This long scene reintroduces Malcolm, affirming his virtues and legitimate claim to the Scottish throne. Macbeth's tyranny is also juxtaposed with the saint-like goodness of the English king (Edward the Confessor), whose divine right to rule makes him blessed with extraordinary powers of healing.

Key point

Macduff and Malcolm conceptualise Scotland as a bloody body, linking blood to physical suffering. This contrasts with Macbeth's understanding of blood as extraneous to the body – as in, 'I am in blood / Stepp'd in so far' (3.4.136–7) – and removed from pain.

The scene is initially preoccupied with the hidden and the unknown. However, its gradual revelation of truths finally propels the action forwards again, and intimates that in the play's resolution the characters will present their true selves to the world.

The revelation of Malcolm's true qualities is followed by a greater focus on Macduff, who initially is ignorant of his family's fate. The impact of the truth shows us another facet to Macduff's personality – his willingness to allow others to see his emotions. Macduff resolves to destroy Macbeth, foreshadowing their final confrontation.

Q What is the significance of King Edward being able to cure his subjects and having 'a heavenly gift of prophecy' (line 159)?

Act 5 Scene 1

Summary: *A Doctor and a Gentlewoman observe Lady Macbeth sleepwalking and talking.*

Guilt-stricken by her complicity in Duncan's murder and by her husband's involvement in the deaths of Banquo, Lady Macduff and others, Lady Macbeth has lost what was once a seemingly formidable strength of mind. Unlike Macbeth, whose madness projects outwards and causes the destruction of others, Lady Macbeth's madness manifests itself inwardly and is therefore self-destructive.

Although immediately after Duncan's murder Lady Macbeth exudes calm, reassuring Macbeth that 'A little water clears us of this deed' (2.2.65), this scene reveals that it is she who suffers most. Her apparent inability to rid her hands of the sight and smell of blood, her sleeptalking and somnambulism (sleepwalking) all work to endorse her belated admission that 'what's done / cannot be undone' (lines 57–8). Her fragility in this scene, combined with her earlier admissions of vulnerability (2.2.1) and regret (3.2.4–7), suggests that her apparent strength was only ever a charade.

Q How do the remarks of the Doctor and the Gentlewoman influence your response to Lady Macbeth in this scene?

Act 5 Scene 2

Summary: *Rebel Scottish lords agree to meet the English near Birnam Wood to fight Macbeth.*

The reference to Birnam Wood recalls the witches' prophecy that Macbeth will reign until Birnam Wood comes to Dunsinane, signalling that Macbeth's demise is imminent.

Macbeth's precarious hold on power is also indicated by the lords' collective animosity towards him. Angus calls Macbeth a 'dwarfish thief' (line 22), and Caithness says Scotland is a 'sickly weal' in need of 'med'cine' (line 27). That Macbeth's soldiers 'move only in command' (line 19) rather than in genuine loyalty to their king is not surprising, nor is the fact that many young men have joined the English forces.

Q Explain how the images of ill-fitting clothes and disease convey the lords' attitudes to Macbeth.

Act 5 Scene 3

Summary: *Macbeth prepares for battle.*

This scene shows Macbeth's struggle to maintain his composure. Although clinging to the belief that he will not be harmed by anyone 'born of woman' (line 4) and insisting to himself that he will 'never sag with doubt nor shake with fear' (line 10), it is clear that Macbeth's hold on power is weakening and that he does have fears and doubts.

The speed with which Macbeth's mood swings between anger and melancholy demonstrates his unhinged psychological state. He accepts that he has 'liv'd long enough' (line 22), but then issues an order to 'Hang those that talk of fear' (line 37). He commands that his armour be put on, then 'Pull't off' (line 55), then 'Bring it after me' (line 59).

Q Is Macbeth regretful of his past actions in this scene, or simply frustrated that he is under attack and greatly outnumbered?

Act 5 Scene 4

Summary: *Malcolm's forces join the soldiers at Birnam Wood.*

As the English forces prepare for battle, Malcolm instructs his men to camouflage themselves behind branches – fulfilling the third prophecy in Act 4 Scene 1. The soldiers are confident, knowing that many of Macbeth's men will not fight for him, emphasising Macbeth's almost complete isolation from his subjects.

Act 5 Scene 5

Summary: *Lady Macbeth dies; Birnam Wood appears to move; Macbeth resolves to fight to the end.*

Although Macbeth's mood continues to change rapidly, he now shows a poignant, reflective quality that we have barely glimpsed since Macduff's flight to England. He realises how accustomed to fears and horrors he has become – 'the initiate fear that wants hard use' (3.5.143) is now all too familiar. Yet he is sufficiently moved by Lady Macbeth's death to meditate on what he now sees as life's brevity and overall insignificance, a profoundly bleak view that clearly derives from the tremendous loss and destruction brought on himself by his own actions.

Macbeth's despair is exacerbated by news that Birnam Wood is moving towards the castle. This confirms his sense that he is a 'poor player' – that his life is 'scripted' by an external force, and nothing he can do will alter its course.

Q Do you think the play as a whole supports Macbeth's assertion that life is 'a tale / … full of sound and fury / Signifying nothing'?

Act 5 Scene 6

Summary: *Malcolm, Siward and Macduff prepare to fight.*

Malcolm's order that the men throw down the branches hastens the plot towards its conclusion. It also signals an end to a time of deception and mistrust: from now on, under Malcolm's rule, people will show their true natures to the world.

Act 5 Scene 7

Summary: *The battle begins; Young Siward is slain.*

Both Macbeth and Macduff are increasingly desperate as their final meeting approaches. Although Macbeth feels trapped, he clings to the prophecy that he is invincible, unable to be harmed by anyone 'of a woman born' (line 14). The ease with which he slays Young Siward reinforces his confidence, and shows once more how assured Macbeth is as a soldier at war.

Unlike Macbeth, Macduff does not kill with abandon. His refusal to kill anyone other than Macbeth conveys his sympathy for the 'wretched Kernes' (foot-soldiers) forced to fight for Macbeth, and emphasises his unwavering desire to avenge the deaths of his wife and children.

Act 5 Scene 8

Summary: *Macbeth and Macduff fight; Macbeth is slain.*

Macbeth's statement that he refuses to play 'the Roman fool' by committing suicide demonstrates his knowledge that his forces will be defeated. He continues to flaunt the notion of his invincibility, but his fright at Macduff's revelation that he was 'from his mother's womb / Untimely ripp'd' (lines 15–16) alerts him to the witches' trickery and temporarily makes him unwilling to fight. Ultimately, though, his pride prompts him to fight valiantly in the face of death – perhaps his first real act of courage since the battle against the Norwegian forces.

Q The slaying of Macbeth is noted in the stage directions rather than by Macduff. How does this impact on your final vision of Macbeth and your understanding of Macduff's character?

Act 5 Scene 9

Summary: *Macduff brings Macbeth's head to Malcolm; Malcolm is hailed as king.*

In some ways this scene ends on a bathetic or anti-climatic note, which is largely a result of Malcolm's relatively bland demeanour. He lacks the plain-spoken directness of Siward, and the natural authority and oratorical flair of Macduff. What Malcolm does have, however, is a measured calmness that Scotland needs after the tumult of Macbeth's reign. His methodical approach to state matters is seen in his final speech, as he works out the immediate tasks at hand. There is the sense that a manager rather than an inspirer of people has come to power: harmony is restored, but a sense of tragic loss is not diminished.

Q Malcolm refers to Macbeth and Lady Macbeth as 'this dead butcher and his fiend-like queen' (line 36). Do we see qualities of Macbeth that are not understood or recognised by the other characters?

CHARACTERS & RELATIONSHIPS

Macbeth

Key quotes

'... brave Macbeth – well he deserves that name –' (Captain, 1.2.16)

'I fear thy nature, / It is too full o'th'milk of human kindness ...' (Lady Macbeth, 1.5.15–16)

'I have no spur / To prick the sides of my intent, but only / Vaulting ambition ...' (1.7.25–7)

'I am in blood / Stepp'd in so far that should I wade no more, / Returning were as tedious as go o'er.' (3.4.136–8)

'Life's but a walking shadow, a poor player / That struts and frets his hour upon the stage / And then is heard no more.' (5.5.23–5)

From the beginning, Macbeth is a man of bold and unflinching action. He is initially a heroic soldier; he becomes a murderer and tyrannical ruler who lives, and finally dies, by the sword. Yet equally – especially for the reader or audience member, who is privy to Macbeth's innermost thoughts – he is defined by his thoughts and feelings, his poetic flair for language, and his capacity to grasp his situation not simply in practical terms, but also in moral and philosophical terms.

Thus, the play enacts not merely a series of murders, but an evolving state of mind. The play's conflict is not merely between Macbeth and those he regards as a threat, but within Macbeth's own consciousness, between what he desires and what he knows is right.

A man of action

Our first knowledge of Macbeth comes from the Captain, who testifies to Macbeth's skill as a swordsman, his fearlessness and his capacity for spontaneous, decisive action. Later, of course, it becomes clear that Macbeth has other qualities – a rich imagination, ambition, a sense of the moral order that underpins society – that give rise to moments of hesitation and vacillation. Yet these moments of anxious indecision also reinforce the degree to which Macbeth is most comfortable when he is acting rather than thinking, when his path does not contain choices or moral questions.

Thus, when Macbeth faces a crisis, his preferred response is to act rather than to reflect. Only on the question of Duncan's murder does his wife need to bring him to the point of action. Subsequently, Macbeth's solution to his state of guilt and fear is to act as he had as a soldier – to recapture that state of absolute certainty and effectiveness attained in the heat of battle. Unfortunately, as Macbeth comes to realise, such a strategy only exacerbates his problems, both practically and psychologically.

Macbeth's moral sense

A key element of Macbeth's complexity is his moral sense, which is conveyed through the doubts he expresses in his soliloquies and much of his early dialogue with Lady Macbeth.

Macbeth's early recognition that murdering Duncan would be wrong in an absolute sense – moral, social, universal – anticipates his later feelings of deep remorse as well as his violent actions. In the powerful soliloquy that begins Act 1 Scene 7, Macbeth conceives of the murder as a perversion not simply of a moral order within society, but of a cosmic order, such that

> pity, like a naked newborn babe
> Striding the blast, or heaven's cherubin hors'd
> Upon the sightless couriers of the air,
> Shall blow the horrid deed in every eye,
> That tears shall drown the wind. (1.7.22–5)

Key point

Here, Macbeth expresses a grasp of his crime's wider context that no other character articulates with such conviction or poetic intensity. For Lady Macbeth the murder is a means to an end; for Macbeth, though, it is a blow against all human feeling, against everything that makes the universe coherent.

In various ways, Macbeth attempts to distance himself from his subsequent actions, as if to avoid their inevitable consequences and, perhaps most significantly, to assuage (lighten) the feelings of guilt and remorse that plague him and rob him of sleep. He insists to Banquo's ghost: 'Thou canst not say I did it' (3.4.50); later he suggests that 'Blood will have blood' (3.4.122), as if it is 'blood' and not himself who is to blame for so much violence. Macbeth is aware of his moral culpability, that is that he is guilty. Yet he continually seeks to deflect responsibility from himself by imagining that the murders he commits (or orders) are due to the mysterious workings of larger, incomprehensible forces – fate, supernatural powers and the apparently self-perpetuating momentum of violence.

Yet the consequences of Macbeth's actions do catch up with him. Banquo's ghost spoils the banquet, Macduff vows to avenge his family's slaughter and Lady Macbeth commits suicide. Finally, he reflects on the apparent meaninglessness of life:

> Life's but a walking shadow, a poor player
> That struts and frets his hour upon the stage
> And then is heard no more. (5.5.23–5)

This speech is an existential cry of despair, triggered by Lady Macbeth's death, but expressing the cumulative effects of fear, unhappiness, destruction and loss.

Key point

One of the core attributes Macbeth has jettisoned (thrown out) in order to transform himself from admired war hero to hated tyrant is his sense of a universal moral order. Previously his actions took place within a universe replete with (full of) significance and meaning – in which stars look on over human affairs and pity might be aroused like 'a naked newborn babe / Striding the blast' (1.7.21–2). In the end, though, Macbeth imagines a meaningless universe no grander in scope than a theatre stage, and views life as fundamentally insignificant, a tale 'Signifying nothing' (5.5.27).

Lady Macbeth

Key quotes

'Come, you spirits / That tend on mortal thoughts, unsex me here / And fill me from the crown to the toe topfull / Of direst cruelty …' (1.5.39–42)

'I have given suck and know / How tender 'tis to love the babe that milks me …' (1.7.54–5)

'Had he not resembled / My father as he slept, I had done't.' (2.2.12–13)

'These deeds must not be thought / After these ways; so, it will make us mad.' (2.2.36–7)

'A little water clears us of this deed. / How easy is it then!' (2.2.70–1)

'Come, come, come, come, give me your hand; what's done cannot be undone.' (5.1.58–60)

Although Lady Macbeth is less fully and complexly drawn than Macbeth, she is one of the great female tragic figures. Like Macbeth, she too falls from a position of power and strength through a flaw in her character, and experiences a tragic demise that arouses the audience's pity in a unique yet powerful fashion.

Sympathy for Lady Macbeth

Our understanding of Lady Macbeth affects how sympathetically we view not only her but Macbeth too. For some readers, Lady Macbeth is no more than an incarnation of evil, and her decline into insanity at the play's end is simply what she deserves. Her declaration that she would have 'dash'd the brains out' of a baby feeding at her breast (1.7.58) is an appalling image and certainly suggests that she lacks compassion or tenderness – or at least that she can ruthlessly suppress such feelings for personal gain. Moreover, she tries to make herself feel *less*: she summons 'spirits / That tend on mortal thoughts' to 'Stop up th'access and passage to remorse' (1.5.39–43). With such a person by his side, we might feel considerable sympathy for Macbeth – who at least expresses doubts about the morality of murdering Duncan.

However, there is much in Lady Macbeth's character to indicate that she is more complex than this, and that she simply suppresses certain feelings in order to help her husband attain the throne. On the night of Duncan's murder she consumes some of the wine she gives the chamberlains, and admits that, as he slept, Duncan reminded her of her own father. She admits these feelings to the audience. However, when Macbeth enters following the murder, she quickly puts aside her nervousness and presents the practical, resilient persona she usually adopts for her husband.

This pattern is repeated when she is queen, a position she has aspired to but which now brings her no pleasure. Early in Act 3 Scene 2 she admits her unhappiness – 'our desire is got without content' (line 5) – but, rather than communicating these feelings to her husband, she focuses on *his* worries. Her attempts to calm Macbeth ('Gentle my lord', line 27) and to dissuade him from thoughts of further murders ('You must leave this', line 35) show her continuing affection and concern for him.

By this point, though, her influence over her husband has virtually ended, and following the disastrous banquet she makes only brief remarks that reflect her weariness and disenchantment. She suggests to Macbeth that he lacks 'the season of all natures, sleep' (line 141), but clearly she, too, lacks sleep, or any other source of solace.

The personal cost of maintaining false appearances

Perhaps no other character is so proficient at 'putting on' a false appearance, yet no character suffers the consequences so severely. Lady Macbeth suggests to her husband that they should appear charming and welcoming hosts to Duncan, and demonstrates all the necessary qualities: in greeting Duncan she is courteous, humble, formal and practical (1.6.15–29). These attributes are evident again at the banquet, when she reminds Macbeth that the feast should be 'given with welcome' (3.4.35).

In reality, of course, she plans the murder of Duncan in her own house and then lives with the uncomfortable knowledge that she is an illegitimate queen. She conceals her unease from all others, including Macbeth, and attempts to convince herself that, with a small effort of the mind, their troubles will fade away. Eventually, though, it becomes clear that her efforts to control her thoughts and feelings after her traumatic experiences have been neither easy, nor ultimately successful. What she has seen and known have indeed affected her deeply – it simply requires the complete breakdown of her personality for it to be revealed.

Memories and knowledge that she tries to suppress end up sending her mad, walking and speaking in her sleep in a way that her conscious mind can no longer control. Things from the past preoccupy her to the exclusion of all else: Duncan's blood remains perpetually on her hands, and her sad recognition that 'what's done cannot be undone' (lines 59–60) suggests that she *would* undo the past if she could. Yet even at this point, her last thoughts remain with her husband, as she seeks once more to comfort him – 'come, give me your hand' (line 59) – and take him to bed.

For more on the play's general treatment of the theme of false appearances, see 'Themes, Ideas & Values'.

Relationship between Macbeth and Lady Macbeth

The intensity and closeness of the relationship between Macbeth and Lady Macbeth gives the first half of the play much of its dramatic tension. It distinguishes both characters from those around them, who are not shown to have equivalent relationships. Only Macduff's wife is represented, and she is portrayed lamenting her husband's absence. In contrast, Macbeth and his wife are constantly exchanging expressions of affection and comfort: 'My dearest love' (1.5.57), 'Gentle my lord' (3.2.27), 'dearest chuck' (3.2.45).

The tension and contrast between them is pronounced in the first two acts. Macbeth's understanding of the immorality of murdering the king causes him to hesitate ('We will speak further', 1.5.70), whereas Lady Macbeth's determination to achieve 'sovereign sway and masterdom' (1.5.69) leads her to become the dominant force in the relationship.

Key point

For Lady Macbeth, power is something that men should want more than anything else, and yet she is the one whose desire for power is the most desperate. She disavows (rejects) female aspects of her identity, since she sees them as preventing her from acting effectively: she wants spirits to 'Come to my woman's breasts / And take my milk for gall' (1.5.46–7). Conversely, she perceives Macbeth's reluctance to act as a sign that he is insufficiently masculine, 'too full o'th'milk of human kindness' (1.5.16). This means that for the first two acts, Macbeth and Lady Macbeth often act and speak in ways that reverse the conventional gender roles of their society.

The conflict climaxes when Lady Macbeth summons all her passion in overturning Macbeth's, 'We will proceed no further' (1.7.31). His objections gradually fade, passing through 'If we should fail?' to 'I am settled' (lines 59 and 79). By the end of this scene they are at their closest, their words and feelings in complete agreement.

Subsequently, they drift apart and their roles reverse. Following the murder, Macbeth immediately grasps that this crime will not easily be left behind, while Lady Macbeth attributes his feelings of guilt and horror to a mental weakness. She instructs him to 'Be not lost / So poorly in your thoughts' (2.2.74–5), as though it is a simple deficiency of willpower that leads to such distress. From this point on, though, it is Macbeth who increasingly spurns thought and commits himself to unhesitating action, whereas Lady Macbeth retreats into introspection and regret.

Her first privately spoken words after becoming queen are: 'Nought's had, all's spent' (3.2.4), echoing Macbeth's 'To be thus is nothing' (3.1.49), but while he seeks the means to be 'safely thus', his wife has little more to give. He conceals his plan to murder Banquo and Fleance from her, in stark contrast to their initial exchanges, in which nothing was held back. She valiantly tries to maintain the appearance of normality at the banquet, but it is her last display of strength.

Macduff

Key quotes

'Here comes the good Macduff.' (Ross, 2.4.20)
Malcolm: Dispute it like a man.
Macduff: I shall do so; / But I must also feel it like a man … (4.3.222–4)
'I have no words; / My voice is in my sword …' (5.8.6–7)

The similarity between the names 'Macbeth' and 'Macduff' points to important correspondences and contrasts between these characters, and it is fitting that their fight brings the play to its conclusion. Both are strong and fearless fighters; both have an independent manner, yet have close family relationships; both express a wide range of emotions.

Macduff's independence

The first signs of Macduff's individuality appear when he is absent from two key occasions: he goes home to Fife rather than to Scone for Macbeth's coronation; and he does not attend Macbeth's banquet, which makes Macbeth suspicious. Others refer to him as 'good Macduff' (Ross, 2.4.20; and Menteith, 5.2.2), yet he is set apart from the other Thanes by his independent behaviour. In contrast to Ross and Lennox, Macduff 'lives in disgrace' (3.6.23).

Malcolm questions Macduff's motives in leaving his 'wife and child' (4.3.26), but gradually his – and our – appreciation of Macduff's integrity and virtue is enhanced. Macduff's 'noble passion' (4.3.114) confirms that his foremost commitment is to Scotland. This establishes a key difference between Macduff and Macbeth, whose primary concern is to hold on to power at any cost.

Notions of manliness

Macduff's distress on learning that all of his family have been killed is conveyed by his initial struggle to speak, and by his balanced response to Malcolm's 'Dispute it like a man' (4.3.222).

Macduff, though, suggests that being a man means being willing to 'dispute' and *also* being able to 'feel it like a man' (4.3.224). Malcolm is pleased that Macduff is prepared to fight – 'This tune goes manly' (4.3.238) – and together they show that necessary balance between feeling and action which has been so lacking under Macbeth's reign of terror.

Malcolm

Key quotes

> 'To show an unfelt sorrow is an office / Which the false man does easy.' (2.3.132–3)
>
> 'I think our country sinks beneath the yoke; / It weeps, it bleeds, and each new day a gash / Is added to her wounds.' (4.3.39–41)

Like Macduff, Malcolm grows in stature as the play approaches its denouement (outcome). He has few lines in the opening scenes, and his first comments following Duncan's murder are quietly to Donaldbain. Both brothers suspect they are in immediate danger, and choose to act cautiously rather than to assert the authority that is rightfully theirs. This caution remains a feature of Malcolm's character, as his initially wary response to Macduff shows (in Act 4 Scene 3). This places him in stark contrast to Macbeth – who barely reflects on the immediate consequences of any of his actions.

Although Malcolm does not at first appear to be a strong leader of men, he gains the support of King Edward and of his 'uncle Siward' (5.2.2), the Earl of Northumberland. He emerges as a shrewder judge of men than his father, and is eventually the logical, as well as the rightful, successor to the throne (see more on Malcolm's leadership under 'The use and abuse of power', p.45).

Nevertheless, Malcolm's speeches lack the poetic flair and expansive vision that characterise Macbeth's, and his summary of Macbeth and Lady Macbeth as 'this dead butcher and his fiend-like queen' (5.9.36) reduces these complex characters to their most heinous deeds. It is clear that Malcolm will restore stability to Scotland, but a more visionary approach is left to those who will succeed him: the descendants of Banquo.

Banquo

Key quotes

> 'Thou hast it now, King, Cawdor, Glamis, all, / As the weïrd women promis'd, and I fear / Thou played'st most foully for't ...' (3.1.1–3)
>
> '... in his royalty of nature / Reigns that which would be fear'd ... He hath a wisdom that doth guide his valour / To act in safety.' (Macbeth, 3.1.51–5)

Banquo is the nearest Macbeth has to a friend or colleague: Banquo refers to a 'most indissoluble tie' between them (3.1.17), which Macbeth ruthlessly severs. Banquo fights heroically alongside Macbeth and, in Duncan's eyes, is as worthy of praise as Macbeth (1.4.30). More importantly, Banquo also encounters the witches, and is the only other lord to know of their prophecies. This gives Banquo a particular insight into the thoughts and actions of his friend.

Banquo's reactions to the prophecies show marked similarities to, and differences from, Macbeth's. Banquo also admits to 'cursed thoughts' (2.1.8) and wonders if the witches can 'set me up in hope' (3.1.10); yet he is always more measured and sceptical in his response. He astutely suspects the witches of being 'instruments of darkness' who wreak havoc by winning their victim's trust 'with honest trifles' (1.3.122–5).

Banquo acts with a calm authority following Duncan's murder: even Macbeth acknowledges Banquo's 'royalty of nature' and 'wisdom that doth guide his valour' (3.1.51–4). However, to Macbeth's disordered mind these qualities appear as threats rather than valuable assets, and he single-mindedly plots the murders of Banquo and Fleance.

Duncan

Key quotes

'Besides, this Duncan / Hath borne his faculties so meek, hath been / So clear in his great office, that his virtues / Will plead like angels ...' (Macbeth, 1.7.16–19)

'Thy royal father / Was a most sainted king ...' (Macduff to Malcolm, 4.3.108–9)

Duncan is universally praised and admired, but his reign is troubled by rebellious lords and his judgement of character is suspect. His declaration that 'There's no art / To find the mind's construction in the face' (1.4.11–12) pinpoints the text's general interest in deceptive appearances, but it also suggests that Duncan lacks the necessary 'arts' of discovering 'the mind's construction' by other means. Moreover, Duncan does little to protect himself from the danger he identifies, and immediately repeats the mistake he has made with Cawdor by rewarding Macbeth with this title and staying at his castle.

Nevertheless, statements by so many – Macbeth's acknowledgement that Duncan has 'been / So clear in his great office' (1.7.17–18); Lennox's lament for 'The gracious Duncan' (3.6.3); and Macduff's reference to 'a most sainted king' (4.3.109) – as well as Duncan's unfailingly regal and courteous manner, testify to his noble character. That is, he sets a moral standard that Macbeth never even hopes to match, and the contrast between the two exposes Macbeth's flawed character even more clearly.

Ross and Lennox

These two lords have very similar roles in the play. Both remain in Scotland throughout Macbeth's violent rule and attempt to retain his trust, though neither participates in Macbeth's acts of violence. They are increasingly critical of Macbeth to others and fully support the uprising led by Malcolm.

Lennox is the more sceptical of the two, and speaks in a cynical, bitter tone to an unnamed Lord (3.6). In contrast, Ross's speech is more wordy and rich in images, exemplified in his portrait of Scotland as a place of 'sighs, and groans, and shrieks that rend the air', where 'good men's lives / Expire before the flowers in their caps' (4.3.170 and 173–4).

Lady Macduff

Although a minor character, Lady Macduff provides an important contrast to Lady Macbeth. Whereas Lady Macbeth demonstrates a passionate commitment to her husband, Lady Macduff appears loyal to her husband while openly questioning his motives. She engages in banter with her son, whereas Lady Macbeth seems incapable of humour and is childless. Lady Macduff thus provides the play's only example of a strong yet nurturing mother – who is then murdered by Macbeth's henchmen.

The scene in which Lady Macduff discusses her absent husband with Ross and then with her son provides a telling instance of how Macbeth's reign of terror impacts on his subjects. Her image of the 'poor wren' that fights to protect her young 'against the owl' (4.2.9–11) encapsulates all the vulnerability and desperation of Scotland's citizens, while also emphasising the importance of protecting the family unit.

THEMES, IDEAS & VALUES

Deceptive appearances

Key quotes

'There's no art / To find the mind's construction in the face.' (Duncan, 1.4.11–12)

'... look like th'innocent flower, / But be the serpent under't.' (Lady Macbeth, 1.5.64–5)

'Where we are, / There's daggers in men's smiles ...' (Donaldbain, 2.3.135–6)

'And make our faces vizards to our hearts, / Disguising what they are.' (Macbeth, 3.2.34–5)

'Though all things foul would wear the brows of grace, / Yet grace must still look so.' (Malcolm, 4.3.23–4)

The question of whether a person's real state of mind is accurately reflected in their outward appearance is at the centre of every exchange and conflict in *Macbeth*. The point is not merely that a person's visual appearance can deceive others; rather, it is that every aspect of how a person presents themselves to the world – their facial expressions, gestures, tone of voice and, above all, what they say – can create a false impression of their real thoughts and feelings. In other words, there is a gap between how a person *seems* to be, and how they really are.

This gap is at the heart of the treachery and fear that pervade the play. The treachery of Cawdor surprises Duncan; Macbeth and Lady Macbeth then vow to appear welcoming and gracious hosts while plotting to murder Duncan in his sleep. Macbeth invites Banquo to a feast he hopes Banquo will never be able to attend, asking seemingly innocent questions about Fleance's whereabouts. Such deception generates widespread mistrust, causing all the characters to speak guardedly and to choose their confidants carefully.

Finally, the conflict is resolved when those characters whose words match their true selves come together, defeating deceit and treachery with honesty and integrity. Malcolm at first asks his men to conceal themselves behind branches, but then – signalling an imminent end to the rule of false appearances – he instructs them to discard their 'leafy screens' and 'show like those you are' (5.6.1–2).

Using appearances to hide real intentions

One of the traits that mark Macbeth and, especially, Lady Macbeth as evil is the calculated way in which they pretend to be good while planning heinous crimes. Lady Macbeth urges her husband not to be so transparent – not to allow his face to be 'a book where men / May read strange matters' – but to 'look like th'innocent flower' (1.5.61–2 and 64). Macbeth becomes more at ease with such deception as he becomes more practised at it. His speeches in response to the discovery of Duncan's body are extravagant in both imagery and length, perhaps reflecting his own genuine remorse, as well as the need, as Lady Macbeth puts it, to 'make our griefs and clamour roar' (1.7.78). However, his later exchange with Banquo shows a new coolness, as he deftly elicits the details of Banquo's ride and Fleance's presence in a natural, conversational manner.

Lady Macbeth encourages the projection of false appearances, but whereas Macbeth immerses himself in a world of violence and deceit – even hiding his actions from his wife – she quickly wearies of such an existence. She urges Macbeth to 'Sleek o'er' his 'rugged looks' and 'be bright and jovial' for their guests (3.2.28), yet at the banquet she 'keeps her state' (3.4.5), remaining on her throne while Macbeth mingles with the guests. She tries to maintain the appearance of normality as his behaviour becomes increasingly erratic, but after she dismisses the guests she says only three more lines in the scene, and then is not seen again until her sleepwalking scene at the start of Act 5.

The cost of deception

The difficulty of telling what is really in people's minds from their appearances is acknowledged throughout the play, and the destruction that follows from Macbeth's treachery and deceit demonstrates the importance of honesty and integrity to the social order. Donaldbain recognises that 'There's daggers in men's smiles' (2.3.136) – meaning not that all men are treacherous, but that it is impossible to tell whose 'smiles' are genuine and whose are merely a facade for more sinister intentions. The guarded manner in which Lennox initially talks to the Lord (3.6) and Malcolm's test of Macduff's honour (4.3) testify to the widespread suspicion and mistrust created by Macbeth's reliance on spies and random acts of violence.

Macbeth also illustrates the costs to the individuals of constantly presenting a 'false face' to the world. The most dramatic instance of this is Lady Macbeth's sleepwalking scene, since her loss of sanity manifests as an inability to mask her inner thoughts from others. Now, what is truly in her mind becomes evident to all who listen; whereas previously she has recommended pushing thoughts of horror and guilt to the back of the mind, now they come to the fore, unable to be governed. It is as if the very effort of burying her guilt is precisely what has driven her mad – the ultimate cost of such deceitfulness.

Key point

A different consequence of living in a world in which false appearances are pervasive is recognised by Macbeth, who attains power without experiencing any of the pleasures or rewards of his position. By the end of the play he retains a small group of supporters, yet he knows that he cannot trust their 'mouth-honour' and their 'breath / Which the poor heart would fain deny' (5.3.27–8). That is, he receives no genuine loyalty and honour, only the appearance of it through falsely spoken words.

Words and equivocation

Just as external appearances can deceive by providing a false impression of a person's true intentions or nature, so too can words in *Macbeth* mislead by having a double meaning. The key term here is equivocation, first introduced in the Porter's speech. On one level this speech is a comic interlude; on another it is a clue to deeper or symbolic meanings – such as the idea of the Macbeths' castle being a hell on earth. The Porter refers to 'an equivocator that could swear in both the scales against either scale' (2.3.8–9), pointing to the use of words to achieve a desired outcome, but not necessarily to express a truth or achieve justice.

The most obvious equivocators in the play are the witches, who speak in such a way that they tell the truth, yet create a false impression for Macbeth about what his reality is actually to be. He thinks his destiny is to achieve greatness, yet his life becomes full of torment and hatred. He thinks he is safe since a wood cannot move from place to place, yet the use of branches as 'leafy screens' (5.6.1) signals his imminent demise. Finally, Macbeth accuses the witches of 'equivocation' (5.5.42) and calls them 'juggling fiends … That palter with us in a double sense'

(5.8.19–20), though each of their prophecies comes true in the course of the play. Macbeth's problem, in a sense, is that he 'reads' their words literally (which gives them the meanings he most wants to hear), whereas their true meaning lies on a metaphorical level.

The use and abuse of power

Key quotes

'Your highness' part / Is to receive our duties, and our duties / Are to your throne and state, children and servants ...' (Macbeth to Duncan, 1.4.23–5)

'I have begun to plant thee and will labour / To make thee full of growing.' (Duncan to Macbeth, 1.4.28–9)

'... this Duncan / Hath borne his faculties so meek, hath been / So clear in his great office ...' (Macbeth, 1.7.16–18)

'He cannot buckle his distemper'd cause / Within the belt of rule.' (Caithness, 5.2.15)

'What's more to do / Which would be planted newly with the time ... by the grace of Grace / We will perform in measure, time and place.' (Malcolm, 5.9.31–40)

Macbeth shows three types – or 'styles' – of leadership through the three characters who are kings of Scotland at different times in the play. The play is framed by the legitimate and seemingly just rule of father and son, Duncan and Malcolm, with Macbeth's tyrannical reign occupying most of the text. However, there are interesting similarities and differences between these three, and through their various responses to conflict and crisis the play explores the strengths and weaknesses of different attitudes to power.

Nurture and the metaphor of planting

While Duncan and Malcolm are obviously linked by their father–son relationship, they share some important leadership qualities. Both use the metaphor of planting and nurturing to convey their understanding of their role as leaders. Duncan greets Macbeth and Banquo not just with praise, but with a promise to help them become even greater. He assures Macbeth he will 'labour / To make thee full of growing' (1.4.28–9), and Banquo continues the metaphor by suggesting the reward or 'harvest' of his own growth would be entirely Duncan's.

Malcolm recalls the language of this exchange in his speech as king which concludes the play. Indeed, he has already signalled that his reign will be more in harmony with the natural world than Macbeth's by using branches from Birnam Wood as camouflage for his army. He knows that there are many things to do 'Which would be planted newly with the time' (5.9.32); like Duncan, he seeks to nurture the state with care and grace. Neither are natural warriors as Macbeth, Banquo and Macduff are, yet they have an air of calm authority and an understanding of the need to gain loyalty through trust rather than terror.

Macbeth, though, lacks the skills and tactical understandings of Malcolm and Duncan, and in contrast wields political power as if he is still in battle. He speaks with some conviction to the two murderers, but clearly has no interest in seeing them 'full of growing': he needs them to remain subservient and compliant. He questions their manhood (as Lady Macbeth had questioned his) and incites them to commit cold-blooded murder. When this is done (although imperfectly, due to Fleance's escape), Macbeth thinks only of his own situation, acknowledging the assassin's work with a curt 'Thanks for that' (3.4.28).

Trust versus caution

If Malcolm as a ruler of people shows more of his father's style than Macbeth does, he also displays a caution in his interactions with others that Duncan seems to have lacked, to his own cost. Not only does Duncan seem completely bewildered by Cawdor's treachery – 'He was a gentleman on whom I built / An absolute trust' (1.4.13–14) – but he makes the same mistake with Macbeth. Duncan is well-loved, but shows none of the instinct for self-preservation that Malcolm has. Indeed, Malcolm's strategy for confirming Macduff's honesty and virtue requires a politician's command of language and a shrewd grasp of human psychology, neither of which Duncan appears to possess. When Macduff learns his wife and children have been murdered, Malcolm – now sure of Macduff's sincerity – prompts him to turn his sorrow into effective action: 'Be this the whetstone of your sword, let grief / Convert to anger' (4.3.231–2).

Macbeth, too, shows an instinctive wariness of the motivations of others, but in his case it is so extreme that it veers towards paranoia. He fears Banquo on the basis of the witches' prophecy, though nothing they say suggests that Banquo poses any immediate threat to Macbeth or his reign. He also mistrusts Macduff for not attending the banquet. Macbeth's fear of being usurped is so strong that he keeps spies in each of the noblemen's houses: 'There's not a one of them but in his house / I keep a servant feed' [bribed] (3.4.131–2). Such constant and pervasive mistrust not only costs Macbeth 'the season of all natures, sleep' (3.4.141), but also generates great resentment and anger among his subjects.

Malcolm, then, represents a pragmatic compromise: he is less trusting and generous than his father, but less brutal and suspicious than Macbeth. He might be less pious than Duncan, and less inspiring and courageous than Macbeth, but he is the one to lead Scotland from turmoil to stability.

Honour

Key quotes

'New honours come upon him / Like our strange garments ...' (Banquo, 1.3.143–4)

'... those honours deep and broad wherewith / Your majesty loads our house.' (Lady Macbeth, 1.6.18–19)

'He hath honour'd me of late, and I have bought / Golden opinions from all sorts of people ...' (Macbeth, 1.7.32–3)

'Macduff, this noble passion ... [has] reconcil'd my thoughts / To thy good truth and honour.' (Malcolm, 4.3.114–17)

'And that which should accompany old age, / As honour, love, obedience, troops of friends, / I must not look to have ...' (Macbeth, 5.3.24–6)

Honour is a quality highly valued in *Macbeth* – its importance to human relationships and the social order is conveyed through the destructive effects of its absence. It is received by individuals who perform good deeds, or whose characters are esteemed. At the start of the play, Duncan is the source of honour: he bestows honour on Macbeth, partly in the form of praise and partly in the form of the title of Thane of Cawdor. He also brings honour to Macbeth and Lady Macbeth by staying at their castle. In return, the noblemen honour their king: as Macbeth says, their duty is to do 'everything / Safe towards [Duncan's] love and honour' (1.5.26–7).

Honour thus involves a set of relationships and a code of conduct, both of which are breached by Duncan's murder. When Macbeth cries 'renown and grace is dead' (2.3.90), he is trying to create a false impression of his shock and distress – but he also accurately identifies the qualities he has discarded. In the world of the play, 'renown' – one's good name or reputation – and 'grace' stem from the king, and underpin the king's capacity to dispense honour and to receive it in turn from his subjects. Macbeth's actions, though, make such an order impossible, since reputations now count for little and there is no infallible source of grace.

The value of honour is linked to the theme of false appearances since honour depends on good words being matched to good intentions. Once it is impossible to distinguish between appearance and reality, it also becomes impossible to decide who is honourable and who is not. Of course, as an audience we can make this distinction, but the characters are caught up in a world in which honour seems to be no more than words spoken in order to please. The Scottish lord to whom Lennox speaks longs for a time when they can once again 'receive free honours' (3.6.36): under Macbeth, 'honours' are compromised by self-interest, and even Macbeth realises that he can only receive 'mouth-honour' (5.3.27). The Messenger who warns Lady Macduff asserts: 'in your state of honour I am perfect' (4.2.63). However, her 'state of honour' depends on her living in a world that recognises and values her status and good name – the Messenger does, but Macbeth does not, and the world he has created has no place for those who embody such a quality.

Since Macbeth has murdered 'renown and grace', Malcolm seeks help from a king who appears to have both in abundance. Edward is 'gracious England' (4.3.43) and it is at his court that Malcolm seeks to re-establish relationships that are based on honour rather than self-interest and deception. He deceives Macduff as to his own nature, pretending to be utterly *dis*honourable in order to elicit Macduff's genuine words of passion for his country. This in turn confirms Macduff's 'truth and honour' (4.3.117), marking the beginning of the restoration of a social order in which honour can once again be freely given and received. Finally, Malcolm is able to bestow honours on his lords, making them earls – 'the first that ever Scotland / In such an honour nam'd' (5.9.30–1).

Fate versus free will

Key quotes

'If chance will have me king, why chance may crown me / Without my stir.' (Macbeth, 1.3.142–3)

'... the golden round, / Which fate and metaphysical aid doth seem / To have thee crown'd withal.' (Lady Macbeth, 1.5.27–9)

'... come Fate into the list, / And champion me to th'utterance.' (Macbeth, 3.1.72–3)

'But yet I'll make assurance double sure / And take a bond of fate ...' (Macbeth, 4.1.82–3)

The idea that certain events in our lives are destined to occur, irrespective of what we choose to do or not to do, runs through *Macbeth* without being conclusively resolved one way or the other. Macbeth's own attitude to fate is contradictory: he believes both that the witches do know the future – that is, that the future is both knowable and fixed – and that he can change that future through his own actions. Nevertheless, the witches' prophecies do all come true, including the unlikely details of Birnam Wood moving to Dunsinane and Macduff not being 'of woman born' (4.1.79 and 5.8.13). Macbeth's sense of being caught up in a course of events that he is relatively powerless to alter gives the play considerable momentum.

The opposing idea is that we are free to determine the course of our lives – that we have free will, are free to choose how to act at any moment, and therefore must bear moral responsibility for our actions. This idea, too, is present throughout the play, since we certainly hold Macbeth accountable for the murders he commits, however much the witches and Lady Macbeth are seen to influence him to begin with. Nor does Macbeth wish to abandon this sense of control over his fate, and he seeks to shape it to his own ends by, for instance, ordering the deaths of Banquo and Fleance.

The other two characters who know about the witches' prophecies – Banquo and Lady Macbeth – are also intensely interested in the idea of fate. Banquo's response is more cautious than Macbeth's, and he is immediately sceptical of the witches' motivations. However, he confesses to 'cursed thoughts that nature / Gives way to in repose'

(2.1.8–9); while Lady Macbeth feels certain that Macbeth will become king since 'fate and metaphysical aid' seem to have him 'crown'd withal' (1.5.28–9). Yet these thoughts are prompted by the witches' words. It is these words that cause certain thoughts and actions, and without them the characters would, it seems, think and act quite differently. In this way, the play leaves open the possibility that it is not fate that determines the characters' actions, but their psychological make-up that leads them in one direction or another.

On the other hand, characters who do not know about the witches are motivated by an altogether different set of qualities. Malcolm and Macduff, for example, are ruled by love of country and allegiance to a code of behaviour that values honour, grace, integrity and truthfulness. Even Macbeth belatedly recognises the value of 'honour, love, obedience, troops of friends' (5.3.25), but it is with a sense of fatefulness, as if such a 'way of life' (5.3.22) was his destiny. In contrast, Malcolm, Macduff, Ross and Lennox never express any sense of resignation to fate; for them, individuals are free to choose, and should always choose in accordance with values that uphold the social and moral order. Seen in this light, Macbeth is always able to choose differently; he simply lets himself be persuaded that his fate 'exists' in some absolute sense. His sense of being a 'poor player', and of life as being no more than a performance on a stage, 'full of sound and fury' but essentially meaningless (5.5.23–7), is, in this view, no more than self-delusion and self-pity. This speech can also be interpreted in other ways; for further discussion, see 'Different Interpretations'.

Key point

Malcolm and those loyal to him are, ultimately, victorious, thus validating the broad view that individuals are not constrained by fate, but are free to act in accordance with their moral sense, to value the well-being of the whole society and to give life meaning and purpose. For more on the play's treatment of fate, see the sample essay near the end of this text guide on the topic '*Macbeth* suggests we have little control over the course of our lives'.

DIFFERENT INTERPRETATIONS

Although the plot of *Macbeth* is quite straightforward, there are many ways of understanding the significance of the various characters and of the play as a whole. The complex motivations and psychological make-up of the central character and the intense, enigmatic relationship between the Macbeths generate many more questions than they answer. Questions about the role that fate might or might not play in our lives, and about the use and abuse of power, are explored without being completely resolved, and remain of enduring interest. (See 'Themes, Ideas & Values'; and the sample answer on the role of fate in the play.)

This section on different ways of interpreting or 'reading' *Macbeth* focuses on the two central characters. It also considers how a performance or adaptation must effectively 'interpret' characters in a particular way through decisions about costume and acting style, about which the text gives few, if any, directions.

Different views of characters

Our reading of the play depends largely on our responses to the two central characters, Macbeth and Lady Macbeth, and to a lesser extent on our response to Macduff and Malcolm. For example, if we see the Macbeths as the embodiment of evil, and Macduff and Malcolm as embodying everything good and wise, then we could 'read' the play as a moral fable about the triumph of good over evil.

However, we could also see Macbeth as a great but flawed man – a courageous warrior with a poet's instinct for language but no talent for ruling a nation – who is replaced by men whose first instinct in times of trouble is to flee the country and plead for assistance. This view might lead to a reading of the play as a critique of absolute power, suggesting that those who gain power rarely have the skills to use it well.

How evil is Lady Macbeth?

One point that has been constantly debated is the degree to which Lady Macbeth is responsible for Macbeth's heinous deeds – particularly the murder of Duncan. Macbeth certainly appears opposed to this deed when he declares 'We will proceed no further in this business' (1.7.31), but Lady Macbeth persuades him otherwise with a mixture of insults and declarations of her own capacity for violence. Her influence is undeniable, but this is not necessarily the same thing as responsibility, and subsequently it is Macbeth rather than his wife who initiates acts of violence.

Moreover, Lady Macbeth does demonstrate a capacity for tender feeling at various points throughout the play, especially when alone on stage, and her decline into madness – when she is no longer able to maintain her steely facade – reveals the human cost of suppressing so much emotion.

Macbeth: villain or victim?

Whereas the question of how sympathetically we view Lady Macbeth tends to focus on whether we see her as cold and calculating, or as feeling the usual range of human emotions, there is much less doubt about Macbeth's emotional range and moral sense. Our view of Macbeth depends more on whether we see him as a tragic victim of circumstances and of a flaw in his character – his ambition – or as a tyrant who willingly and ruthlessly terrorises his people.

The following two key moments are open to different views of Macbeth's character and motivations. There is no 'right' or 'wrong' way of interpreting such scenes (and there are others that could also be selected), but avoid seeing them in isolation; your overall interpretation should apply to the play as a whole.

- **The argument between Macbeth and Lady Macbeth about whether or not to murder Duncan** (1.7.31–82) – does this scene reveal Macbeth to be a fundamentally weak and gullible figure who readily submits to his wife's demands? Or does she simply overcome Macbeth's self-doubts and allow him to accomplish what he initially wanted to?
- **Macbeth's speech following the death of Lady Macbeth** (from 'She should have died hereafter', 5.5.16–27) – is this a lament for Lady Macbeth, a cry of anguish about his own desperate situation or a profound insight into the human condition? Does the play ask us to agree with Macbeth's bleak view of life, or does the speech simply convey Macbeth's distorted perspective?

Performance and adaptation

The many film and television versions of Macbeth suggest interestingly diverse ways of thinking about the characters. For example, in a television adaptation for the BBC's ShakespeaRe-Told series, relocated and updated to a contemporary Glasgow restaurant, the Duncan character is portrayed as exploitative and arrogant, shifting audience sympathies towards the Macbeths.

Although this characterisation is more a product of the scriptwriter's reworking of the original text than anything Duncan actually says in the play, it reminds us that we know almost nothing about Duncan, and that much of his demeanour and personality is left to the actor to 'flesh out' in performance. A quite different 'Duncan' is represented in Trevor Nunn's production, dressed entirely in white and initially seen praying fervently. This pious Duncan is not inconsistent with the text – which the performance follows exactly – but again the costume, actions and manner are creations of the director, costume designer and actor rather than of the written word.

QUESTIONS & ANSWERS

This section focuses on your own analytical writing on the text, and gives you strategies for producing high-quality responses in your coursework and exam essays.

Essay writing – an overview

An essay on a literary work is a formal and serious piece of writing that presents your point of view on the text, usually in response to a given topic. Your 'point of view' in an essay is your interpretation of the meaning of the text's language, structure, characters, situations and events, supported by detailed analysis of textual evidence.

Analyse – don't summarise

In your essays it is important to avoid simply summarising what happens in a text.

- A **summary** is a description or paraphrase (retelling in different words) of the characters and events. For example: 'Macbeth has a horrifying vision of a dagger dripping with blood before he goes to murder King Duncan.'
- An **analysis** is an explanation of the real meaning or significance that lies 'beneath' the text's words (and images, for a film). For example: 'Macbeth's vision of a bloody dagger shows how deeply uneasy he is about the violent act he is contemplating, and conveys his sense that supernatural forces are impelling him to act.'

A limited amount of summary is sometimes necessary to let your reader know which part of the text you wish to discuss. However, always keep this to a minimum and follow it immediately with your analysis of what this part of the text is really telling us.

Plan your essay

Carefully plan your essay so that you have a clear idea of what you are going to say. The plan ensures that your ideas flow logically, that your argument remains consistent and that you stay on the topic. An essay plan should be a list of **brief dot points** – no more than half a page.

Include your central argument or main contention – a concise statement (usually in a single sentence) of your overall response to the topic. See 'Analysing a Sample Topic' for guidelines on how to formulate a main contention.

Write three or four dot points for each paragraph indicating the main idea and evidence/examples from the text. Note that in your essay you will need to *expand* on these points and *analyse* the evidence.

Structure your essay

An essay is a complete, self-contained piece of writing. It has a clear beginning (the introduction), middle (several body paragraphs) and end (the last paragraph or conclusion). It must also have a central argument that runs throughout, linking each paragraph to form a coherent whole. See examples of introductions and conclusions in the 'Analysing a Sample Topic' and 'Sample Answer' sections.

The introduction establishes your overall response to the topic. It includes your main contention and outlines the main evidence you will refer to in the course of the essay. Write your introduction *after* you have done a plan and *before* you write the rest of the essay.

The body paragraphs argue your case – they present evidence from the text and explain how this evidence supports your argument. Each body paragraph needs:

- a strong **topic sentence** (usually the first sentence) that states the main point being made in the paragraph
- **evidence** from the text, including some brief quotations
- **analysis** of the textual evidence, with **explanation** of its significance and how it supports your argument
- **links back to the topic** in one or more statements, usually towards the end of the paragraph.

Connect the body paragraphs so that your discussion flows smoothly. Use some linking words and phrases such as 'similarly' and 'on the other hand', though don't start every paragraph like this. Another strategy is to use a significant word from the last sentence of one paragraph in the first sentence of the next.

Use key terms from the topic – or synonyms for them – throughout, so the relevance of your discussion to the topic is always clear.

The conclusion ties everything together and finishes the essay. It includes strong statements that emphasise your central argument and provide a clear response to the topic.

Avoid simply restating the points made earlier in the essay – this will end on a very flat note and imply that you have run out of ideas and vocabulary. The conclusion should be a logical extension of what you have written, not just a repetition or summary of it. Writing an effective conclusion can be a challenge. Try using these tips:

- Start by linking back to the final sentence of the second-last paragraph – this helps your writing to flow, rather than leaping back to your main contention straight away.
- Use synonyms and expressions with equivalent meanings to vary your vocabulary. This allows you to reinforce your line of argument without being repetitive.
- When planning your essay, think of one or two broad statements or observations about the text's wider meaning. These should be related to the topic and your overall argument. Keep them for the conclusion, since they will give you something 'new' to say but still follow logically from your discussion. The introduction will be focused on the topic, but the conclusion can present a wider view of the text.

Essay topics

1. 'Lady Macbeth is the real villain of the play.'
   Do you agree?
2. 'It is the witches and Lady Macbeth who are responsible for Macbeth's downfall.'
   Discuss.
3. Malcolm refers to Macbeth and Lady Macbeth as "this dead butcher and his fiend-like queen".
   How accurate is Malcolm's view of these characters?
4. Macbeth states that: "nothing is but what is not".
   'Macbeth is entirely responsible for his country's state of chaos and fear.'
   Discuss.

5 'Macbeth is a tyrant, but he never loses his noble qualities.'
Discuss.

6 "I have no spur / To prick the sides of my intent, but only / Vaulting ambition ..."
Is Macbeth's ambition his only weakness?

7 "Life's but a walking shadow ..."
'*Macbeth* presents a bleak view of life.'
Do you agree?

8 "Things bad begun, make strong themselves by ill."
'The play shows that those who come to power by violent means inevitably rule by violent means.'
Discuss.

9 '*Macbeth* suggests we have little control over the course of our lives.'
Discuss.

10 '*Macbeth* shows that there can be no justice in a society ruled by violence and fear.'
Discuss.

Analysing a sample topic

'Lady Macbeth is the real villain of the play.' Do you agree?

This question looks simple but has some underlying complexities, and it is important to avoid writing an essay that is just a list of Lady Macbeth's evil qualities. Such a response would be repetitive and would not really answer the question.

The first two things to consider are:

- what do we mean by 'villain'?
- who else could be considered the 'real villain'?

The answer to the second question would probably be Macbeth, although you might point to the witches or a combination of both. The important point is that the topic is really asking you to *compare* Lady Macbeth's actions to those of Macbeth (and possibly the witches) in order to determine who is the *real* – that is, the worst or most destructive – villain in the play.

The meaning of 'villain' could be something like this: 'a character whose actions deliberately cause pain and suffering to those who are innocent and good'. An important element to think about is the character's state of mind. How crucial is their sense of compassion for their victims, or their moral sense? Is a character villainous simply because of their actions, or do their underlying feelings make them more or less of a villain?

A key feature of the play is the way in which the roles of Macbeth and Lady Macbeth 'swap' following the murder of Duncan. At first it seems that Lady Macbeth has all the most evil and amoral qualities, and without her persuasive powers Macbeth would never proceed with the murder. In the second half of the play, though, Macbeth becomes ruthless and unfeeling, whereas Lady Macbeth feels increasingly guilty and remorseful. This shift in power makes it difficult to identify one or the other as the 'real villain', and should be addressed in any response to this topic.

Introduction

In your introduction, clearly state your response to the topic: you can agree, disagree or partially agree/disagree with the topic. Whichever position you take, needs to be justified with an overall reason – this is your main contention or argument. For example:

- *Agreement:* 'Lady Macbeth is the real villain of the play because without her, Macbeth would never murder Duncan and become a violent dictator.'
- *Disagreement:* 'Lady Macbeth is not the real villain, since it is not her actions but Macbeth's that cause the disintegration of Scotland's social order.'
- *Partial agreement:* 'Lady Macbeth and Macbeth are both villains, but neither is more responsible than the other for the terror and violence of their reign.'

The introduction should also indicate the main pieces of textual evidence you will use in the body paragraphs to support your overall argument.

Body paragraphs: textual evidence

The following points identify some key moments in the text that you can use to develop your discussion. Look to include short, effective quotations: these support your argument and demonstrate your close knowledge of the text. Make sure you consider the *meaning* of each scene you refer to – don't assume that its relevance to the topic or to your response will be obvious to the reader.

- In Act 1 Scene 5, Lady Macbeth deliberately suppresses her capacity to feel in order to accomplish the murder of Duncan. She wants to become full of 'direst cruelty' and to 'Stop up th'access and passage to remorse' (lines 42 and 43). That is, she wants to cast aside her very humanity, and to feel nothing for those who suffer as result of her actions.
- In Act 1 Scene 7, Macbeth determines that he will 'proceed no further in this business' (line 31). Only Lady Macbeth's passionate speeches change his mind. Whereas Macbeth raises convincing moral objections to the murder, she questions his 'valour' (line 40) and asserts her own unflinching capacity for violence – and for suppressing any tender feeling. In this scene, at least, she is much more the villain than Macbeth.
- However, later events show that she is not as bold and immune to feeling as she claims to be. Consider her admissions to the audience – though not to Macbeth – that Duncan 'resembled' her own father (2.2.12) and 'our desire is got without content' (3.2.5). She presents a particular personality to her husband, but the reality underneath is rather different.
- Lady Macbeth instigates and plans Duncan's murder, but she never indicates that she wishes to continue in this way. Once she is queen she seeks to calm Macbeth and discourage thoughts of further murders ('You must leave this', 3.2.35).
- Macbeth, however, becomes less sympathetic once he becomes king. Previously he had given weight to values such as honour and trust ('He's here in double trust', 1.7.12), but these fade into the background as fears overwhelm him and he begins to murder all those he regards as potential threats. This violent course of action could be interpreted in two ways:
    - Macbeth emerges as the real villain of the play, using excessive violence and planting spies throughout Scotland in order to deprive his subjects' lives of peace and trust.

   - Macbeth is caught up in circumstances initially created by Lady Macbeth (and to some extent by the witches): he feels that violence has its own logic ('Blood will have blood', 3.4.122) and he is unable to return to a peaceful state. In this interpretation, Lady Macbeth remains the real villain since she is the 'architect' of subsequent events.
- Consider Lady Macbeth's sleepwalking scene (5.1). Does her decline into madness, full of horror and remorse, make her less of a villain?

Conclusion

The conclusion must draw together the evidence presented in the body paragraphs and reiterate the overall argument.

- Try to vary your word choices – avoid a simple repetition of words and phrases from topic sentences.
- Aim to end with a strong statement responding to the topic, but avoid ending with a quotation, since this can leave the reader wondering what is really meant.

SAMPLE ANSWER

'*Macbeth* suggests we have little control over the course of our lives.' Discuss.

From Macbeth's first appearance in the play until his last, it seems as if the course of his life is already determined. The witches appear to have knowledge of future events in Macbeth's life, and each of their prophecies is fulfilled, including the specific 'none of woman born / Shall harm Macbeth'. This creates the impression that the future is as fixed and decided as the past, and that individuals struggle against their destiny in vain. Yet Macbeth struggles not against supernatural forces, but with problems entirely of his own making: the murder of Duncan, the ruthless slaughter of innocents, the terrifying of an entire country, all have consequences that he tries, but fails, to control. In this way, *Macbeth* leaves the question of whether we can control the course of our lives unresolved, while demonstrating the power of individuals to make choices that impact not just on their own lives but on those of the whole society.

The witches' knowledge that Macbeth has been named Thane of Cawdor certainly gives him – and the audience – the sense that the future can be known, and that the witches have access to such knowledge. However, their prediction that he will become king does not include any reference to murder – this idea is entirely his and Lady Macbeth's creation. Moreover, it is the very act of telling Macbeth that he will become king that sets in motion the chain of thoughts that leads Macbeth to the throne. Macbeth is entirely free to ignore the witches, and to treat Duncan as a revered king and honoured guest. If his life's course is truly predetermined, and the witches are correct, this would bring him to the throne just as surely as an act of regicide. By showing the dramatic impact of the prophecies on Macbeth's mental state, and his almost immediate thoughts of murder, the play leaves open the question of whether it is fate, or our own free choices, that control the course of our lives.

Lady Macbeth and Banquo are also affected by the witches' prophecies, but they respond in quite different ways – further emphasising the role of individual character and choice. Banquo is intrigued by the prospect of being 'the root and father / Of many kings', yet he is not moved to violent action as Macbeth and Lady Macbeth are. In fact, Lady Macbeth's response is quite contradictory: she suggests that 'fate and metaphysical aid doth seem / To have thee crown'd withal' – that is, that no definite action on her part is required – yet she regards the murder of Duncan as a matter of urgency. She summons 'spirits / That tend on mortal thoughts' to make her full of 'direst cruelty', but there is no suggestion that this appeal is successful, or that she is capable of committing murder herself. Her only reference to this possibility comes after she has seen Duncan sleeping, and found herself moved by his close resemblance to her own father. In this, Lady Macbeth asserts her capacity to choose, and thus demonstrates her underlying humanity, rather than the power of supernatural forces over her life.

Finally, Macbeth returns to the witches 'to know / By the worst means, the worst'. Yet even he cannot relinquish the sense that he might act in a way that will improve his chances of survival. Once again, the witches' prophecies actually shape Macbeth's subsequent actions – thus, these actions are as readily explained in psychological terms as metaphysical ones. That Macduff is not 'of woman born' lends weight to the notion that our fates are predetermined. Yet even in this the prophecy is open-ended, signalling only that 'harm' will come to Macbeth. But what kind of harm? That Macduff ultimately kills Macbeth could, within the world of the play, be due to external forces over which individuals have no control. It is just as plausible, however, that it results from the entirely controllable and understandable forces of human emotions and impulses.

Although the witches seem to have access to more than 'mortal knowledge', the play does not conclusively demonstrate that such knowledge means our lives are predetermined. The witches' prophecies themselves play a large part in determining the course of lives in the play, and characters act not for inexplicable reasons, but for quite natural ones – such as ambition, fear and revenge. Macbeth sees his destiny before him – but then he proceeds to forge his own destiny, constructing his own tragic demise. In this way, the question of what determines the fates of human beings is left unresolved. It is, rather, the struggle of human beings against what they perceive as their destiny that the play explores with such horror, pity and compassion.

REFERENCES & READING

Text

Shakespeare, William 2001, *Macbeth*, Oxford School Shakespeare, Oxford University Press, Oxford.

Criticism and background

Barnet, Sylvan 1963, 'Introduction' to *Macbeth*, Signet Classics, New York, pp.xxii–xxxiii.

Bradley, AC 1957, 'Lecture IX' and 'Lecture X' in *Shakespearean Tragedy*, Macmillan, London. First published 1904.

Dunton-Downer, Leslie & Alan Riding 2004, *Essential Shakespeare Handbook*, Dorling Kindersley (DK), London.

Film and television adaptations

The Tragedy of Macbeth 2021, dir. Joel Coen.

Macbeth 2015, dir. Justin Kurzel.

Macbeth 2010, dir. Rupert Goold.

Macbeth 2006, dir. Geoffrey Wright.

Set in the present-day Melbourne underworld, using the original language.

Macbeth 1983, dir. Jack Gold.

Television version for the BBC Television Shakespeare series; very faithful to the text.

Macbeth 1978, dir. Philip Casson.

A television version of Trevor Nunn's stage production for the Royal Shakespeare Company.

The Tragedy of Macbeth 1971, dir. Roman Polanski.

Perhaps the most famous film version of Macbeth, *emphasising the violent nature of Macbeth's reign.*

Throne of Blood 1957, dir. Akira Kurosawa.

Celebrated adaptation set in Feudal Japan.

Website

Shakespeare Online, www.shakespeare-online.com

See the article 'Shakespeare's Sources for Macbeth*' for an overview of how Shakespeare used various sources for the play.*

IMPROVE YOUR VOCABULARY

Here is a list of key words for analysing and writing about *Macbeth*. These words appear throughout this text guide. You should aim to use these words in your essays. We have provided a page reference to an example of how each word can be used.

accoutrements	p.24
allegiance	p.14
assuage	p.33
belies	p.18
circumspection	p.17
complicity	p.24
conveys	p.20
deferential	p.19
demise	p.16
disavows	p.37
disquietude	p.20
equivocation	p.44
harrowing	p.21
hubris	p.7
inextricably	p.9
inverts	p.11
malevolence	p.17
pertinent	p.10
pervasive	p.47
precarious	p.17
prevalence	p.9
public persona	p.10
regicide	p.7
renown	p.48
reticence	p.22
signifies	p.9
traitorous	p.16
tyranny	p.27
uncanny	p.12
usurping	p.4
vulnerability	p.28